MW00608719

The Art of the
CYCLING JERSEY

The Art of the
CYCLING JERSEY

ICONIC CYCLE WEAR / PAST AND PRESENT

CHRIS SIDWELLS

Author of A Race for Madmen

RODALE.

RODALE
wellness

Live happy. Be healthy. Get inspired.

Sign up today to get exclusive access to our authors, exclusive bonuses, and the most authoritative, useful, and cutting-edge information on health, wellness, fitness, and living your life to the fullest.

Visit us online at RodaleWellness.com
Join us at RodaleWellness.com/Join

Mention of specific companies, organizations, or authorities in this book does not imply endorsement by the author or publisher, nor does mention of specific companies, organizations, or authorities imply that they endorse this book, its author, or the publisher. Internet addresses and telephone numbers given in this book were accurate at the time it went to press.

© 2016 Quid Publishing

Photography and illustration credits appear on page 224

All rights reserved. No part of this publication may be reproduced or transmitted in any form or by any means, electronic or mechanical, including photocopying, recording, or any other information storage and retrieval system, without the written permission of the publisher.

Rodale books may be purchased for business or promotional use or for special sales. For information, please write to: Special Markets Department, Rodale, Inc., 733 Third Avenue, New York, NY 10017

Bicycling is a registered trademark of Rodale Inc.

Printed and bound in China by C&C Offset Printing Co., Ltd

Book design by Lindsey Johns

Library of Congress Cataloging-in-Publication Data
is on file with publisher.

ISBN 978-1-62336-737-4 hardcover

Distributed to the trade by Macmillan

2 4 6 8 10 9 7 5 3 1 hardcover

RODALE

We inspire health, healing, happiness, and love in the world.
Starting with you.

Contents

Foreword

The bicycle and the body of the bicyclist are the two most essential components of the quality that might be considered something as simple as style but could also be described as presence, state, or even haecceity. I'm talking about that specific "rider-ness" each of us has, which comes from or creates (or, probably, both) how we sit a bike, how we pedal, how much and in which ways we lean ourselves and our bicycles through corners, how we hold the bike, how we balance it beside us as we walk, how we handle it as we hang it on a hook or push it through a door or shoulder it up a staircase—any time we are in communion with our bicycle.

Of the rest of the elements that make us "us," I put the cycling jersey an easy third to bike and body. What's more, in terms of range of expressiveness, I put it first. The jersey! The most dominant value of the cycling aesthetic, and one of its simplest components, yet also the one most laden with subtext and potential ironies and sincerities and affiliations and memories and references often unknown to the wearer. A jersey can be a nod to a team, a racer, an era, a fabric, a design sense, a remembrance, a personal experience, an aspiration, or else simply come in a color we really really like and that happened to be in our size. One can, for instance, wear and cherish a Molteni jersey for the distinct and odd color, without knowing anything about Eddy Merckx; or, if one knows Merckx, remaining ignorant of the grand loyal domestique Jos Huysmans; or, fully immersed in racing history, forget that Molteni was a sausage factory and lose out on the delicious pleasure of that contradiction. And how to even begin comprehending the Brooklyn jersey, the vestment of an Italian chewing gum company in an All-American design, and best and most nobly worn by a Belgian known as "Monsieur Paris–Roubaix" for his otherworldly career record in a quintessentially Flandrian race that never leaves France. (It is said that Roger De Vlaeminck never suffered a flat tire on the cobbles until he forsook the Brooklyn jersey late in his career.)

So it is that a jersey influences how others regard you, from the simplest observations (how pretty), to philosophical judgments that may be far beyond your own ken. But the jersey also influences its rider, I believe. It tells us who we are on a bike and who we might be and who we don't care to be, and it helps us get to whichever of those destinations it is that we have chosen to prize, and it helps us, as well, get what we need to arrive there. This volume is a wonderland for those who appreciate all that, and a door to that world for those who don't yet, but might.

A lithographic print produced in Detroit in 1895, at a time when cycling as a spectator sport was rapidly gaining popularity.

Bill Strickland
Editor-in-chief, *Bicycling* magazine
July, 2016

Introduction

This book traces the development of the cycling jersey from the jackets and woolen pullovers worn by early racers, to the sophisticated designs and materials that make up the very latest cycling jerseys today. It tells the story of the jerseys awarded to champions, and those that denote the leaders of the various competitions of the Grand Tours—the Tour de France, Giro d'Italia, and Vuelta a España. These jerseys are iconic, but so are those of the professional teams that the best riders in the history of cycling have raced for.

The French national team pictured at the 1932 Tour de France. From left to right: André Leducq, Albert Barthélémy, Julien Momeau, Louis Peglion, Marcel Bidot, Maurice Archambaud, Georges Speicher, and Roger Lapébie.

The most iconic cycling jerseys possess a mystique and a beauty that is a distillation of their design and the part they played in the sport. Professional teams have a very important place in the story of the cycling jersey, as do the riders, and *The Art of the Cycling Jersey* reveals facts about some of the famous, and not so famous, characters who have brought fame and glory to their jerseys—from the Bianchi team jersey worn by Fausto Coppi, the Molteni of Eddy Merckx, and the St. Raphaël of Jacques Anquetil to the Tebag of Ferdi Kübler and the EMI of Charly Gaul.

From the maiden Tour de France in 1903 (see the photo on page 5) and the very first pro team jerseys, such as Thomann–Dunlop and Automoto–Hutchinson, we follow the sport's evolution up until modern times and the design standouts of Carrera,

Jacques Anquetil, Eddy Merckx and Felice Gimondi photographed in 1970; all three won the Tour de France.

Mapei, and ONCE. There is also a separate chapter dedicated to the story of the six-day jersey. An offshoot of mainstream cycling, six-day races have a long and fascinating history, and they have jersey traditions of their own. The stories of these and many more jerseys are told in this book.

But this book is not just a celebration of iconicity. It explains the ways in which cycling jerseys have developed over the years. As professional cycling changed, so did the type of businesses that sponsored the teams, and those businesses have been responsible for jersey designs, because they want something that best reflects their brand.

Finally, this book reflects the broad-brushstrokes history of Europe from around the turn of the 20th century, through two

World Wars, and up to the present day. For example, when Europe went through the interwar years of rampant nationalism, so the Tour de France switched from trade-sponsored to national teams with national team jerseys. Then after the Second World War, as the continent grew more affluent, the sponsorship of cycling teams changed from bicycle manufacturers to a wider range of businesses.

As well as celebrating the cycling jersey, this book tells its story, and the stories of the people who played a part in it. That story continues today, with a better understanding of cycling and new materials making modern cycling jerseys not just good to look at and wear, but really technical pieces of high-performance gear.

Competitors at the Porte
Maillot in Paris for the start
of the first ever Paris-Roubaix
race, held on April 19, 1896.
The start choice is a happy
coincidence, as *maillot* is
the French word for
"cycling jersey."

THE CYCLING JERSEY IS BORN

This chapter looks at the first clothes cyclists used for racing, and traces how they changed over time, from adapted street clothing to cycling-specific gear, which resulted in the birth of the cycling jersey.

Early Cycling Clothing

1868—1900

Cycling clothing, such as plus-fours and knickerbockers, and jackets with longer sleeves, appeared as soon as cycling became popular in the 1860s and '70s. The first racers wore similar garments, although they were lighter and a little more streamlined than those used for everyday cycling. Rudimentary velodromes were constructed for racing, and track cycling became really popular. As it evolved, track racers wore sleeker clothing, shorts, and tight tops.

THE FIRST RACE

It's possible that there were other bike races before May 31, 1868—in fact, there were other races held in the Parc St. Cloud in Paris that day—but it's the 1-kilometer (0.63 mile) race, won by a British cyclist, James Moore, that is the most talked about, and the most written about. It was probably the main event on a card of races that was organized by the Olivier brothers, who were pioneer bike manufacturers from the Compagnie parisienne des vélocipèdes.

Moore, who was born in Suffolk, England, and moved to Paris with his parents, won the race on a boneshaker wooden bike, which had iron tires, at an average speed of 14.4 miles per hour (23.2 kph). He was wearing plus fours and a shirt and tie, with a buttoned jacket. Dashing attire, topped off with a shallow, open-crown round-brimmed hat.

Moore also won the first place-to-place road race, Paris to Rouen, on November 7, 1869. He was on his boneshaker bike again, taking 10 hours 45 minutes for the 76 miles (129 km), and his clothing was very similar to what he wore for the Parc St. Cloud race, except his jacket was finished with braided pockets and lapels.

Male leisure cyclists wore normal clothing in the late 1880s, but some women wore knickerbockers, which was an important step in the emancipation movement.

Riders in this 1886 race at the Alexandra Palace in London are wearing some of the first clothing designed for cycle racing.

TRACK CYCLING

Despite the efforts of Moore in France and people like John Mayall junior, who set place-to-place records in England, road racing didn't really catch the public's imagination at first. They preferred to watch racing on prepared cinder tracks.

This kind of racing was especially popular in the UK. In an effort to make the racing faster and more entertaining, the size of the front wheel was increased (the pedals of early bikes were attached directly to the front wheel, meaning that a larger front wheel would allow a greater distance to be covered by each pedal revolution). The result was the penny-farthing bike, which had a huge front wheel and a tiny back one.

For their Varsity match on June 16, 1874, which was held on the Lillie Lane cinder track in London, Oxford's H.P. Whiting and the Hon. Ion Keith Falconer of Cambridge wore white cotton knickerbockers with long woollen socks and long-sleeved woollen vests.

Whiting beat Falconer in a 25-mile (40-km) race, recording a time of 1 hour 41 minutes and 16.5 seconds (Victorians were sticklers for exact timing). His winning margin was 100 yards (91 m), and the victory was quite a surprise, considering the shorter Whiting rode a penny-farthing with a 54-inch (137-cm) front wheel, while the much taller Falconer's bike had a 60-inch (152-cm) front wheel.

At first, track cycling was a sport for the wealthy, but professional racers soon took over from amateurs such as Whiting and Falconer, especially after the invention of the chain-driven safety cycle. With a chain-driven bike, speed depended more on the rider's fitness, strength, and determination, and less on the length of his legs. Furthermore, the big cash prizes on offer in some races, plus the growth of betting, created a financial incentive for tough working-class athletes, who were highly motivated to make money.

Racers were split into sprinters and stayers, and crowds flocked to see sprint speed merchants and powerful stayers, who were often paced in their races by tandems, then triplets and quadruplets, all in the name of increasing the speed, the danger, and the spectacle.

Riders at the start of a track race for penny-farthing bikes in Niagara Falls in the USA. Early track races like this were fast, but became more so with the invention of the chain-driven bike.

Track racing became popular throughout Europe and the United States, with riders like the American A.A. Zimmerman, Constant Huret and Edmond Jacquelin of France, and the Englishman Frank Shorland making a fortune from racing in front of packed crowds on both sides of the Atlantic.

These track racers wore wool shorts and vests, which were much more body-hugging and aerodynamic than the clothing road cyclists wore at the time. Track cycling also gave the world its first African-American sports star. His name was Marshall Walter Taylor.

MAJOR TAYLOR

Taylor was born in Indiana in 1878 and was the first African-American world champion in cycling and only the second black man to win a world title in any sport, after the Canadian boxer George Dixon.

Taylor's first job, when he was 12 years old, was to perform bike tricks outside a Chicago bike shop while wearing a soldier's uniform. It earned him the nickname "Major." He started racing on the road at 16, and it wasn't long before he was winning, but it was on the track that his blistering sprint served him best.

Taylor became a professional at 18 and was soon beating everyone in America. In 1899 he set a new world record. Riding behind a tandem, he took 1 minute and 18 seconds to cover 1 mile (1.6 km). That's 45.56 miles per hour (73.32 kph). He later won the world championship in Montreal over half a mile (0.8 km). In 1902 he was contracted to ride 57 races in Europe and he won 40 of them. Major Taylor continued winning races and breaking records, as well as the barriers of racism, until 1910, when he retired from racing.

Major Taylor riding an early chain-driven track bike. His low crouch, tucked-in elbows, and figure-hugging woolen outfit all improved his aerodynamics.

At his peak, Taylor looked surprisingly like a modern track cyclist. His cycling clothes were made from wool, but they were always tight-fitting and very aerodynamic. He raced in long-and short-sleeved jerseys, even sleeveless ones, and there are pictures of him wearing what looks like a one-piece knitted cycling suit, rather like the skinsuits track racers wear today.

His outfits were always brightly colored, but the most flamboyant was a white top with a blue collar and sleeves, which he wore with skin-tight blue shorts that had a contrasting ring around each leg. Knotted around his middle Taylor wore a Stars and Stripes flag.

Maurice Garin's White Cotton Jacket

1903

Maurice Garin won the first-ever Tour de France in 1903. In those days, racers didn't ride in teams, so they were free to choose their own clothing. Some wore shorts, and some wore tights on their legs, while on top they had a light undershirt, with sweaters or jackets over this. For the 1903 Tour de France Maurice Garin raced mostly in a distinctive white jacket. Once he led the race, after winning the marathon first stage of 292 miles (467 km) from Paris to Lyon, the organizers gave him a green armband to wear as race leader.

Maurice Garin, winner of the first Tour de France in 1903, poses with his bike. His choice of white tops not only made him stand out to spectators, but also helped him stay cool.

Maurice Garin was born in the Aosta Valley in northwest Italy, but moved with his family to northern France out of economic necessity during his early teens. Rural Italy was poor, and there was work in France's industrial north, but the free movement of labor through Europe wasn't allowed. Garin's father had to smuggle his family out of Italy in ones and twos, which gave rise to some myths that emerged as Maurice became famous.

One of these was that his father swapped Maurice for a whole cheese. If a cheese did change hands, it was probably payment for transporting Maurice north. The other myth, which claims that Garin worked as a chimney sweep, is partly true. He did work as a sweep for a very short time, while passing through Reims on his way north, but kids were smuggled through networks and again, young Garin's work was probably a means of payment for that.

Eventually, though, he made it north, started cycling, took French nationality, and became a pro racer in 1893. Garin was good and he won most of the big races of his day, including Paris–Roubaix, which he won twice.

THE FIRST TOUR

There were six stages in the first Tour de France, each of them a few days apart to give stragglers time to finish one and recover for the next, and they were huge. Four of the six stages were over 250 miles (400 km), and the shortest was 168 miles (268 km). The winner of that stage, Charles Laeser, took 8 hours 46 minutes to cover the distance, while the last man, Arsène Millocheau, took over 14 hours.

Early cycling jackets were made of cotton or Alpaca wool, the cotton often waxed as a partial means of waterproofing. Sweaters were made from wool yarn, which kept its shape quite well and would soak up sweat to some extent, giving the riders a degree of comfort.

Jackets had large hip pockets and could be buttoned up as far as the neck. Sweaters also had pockets stitched onto the chest area. Rear pockets in pullovers were a later addition. It was the sweater that evolved slowly into the more familiar racing jersey.

The first cycling jerseys were plain wool, but bicycle manufacturers who sponsored early professional riders soon saw the publicity possibilities of having their names on the jerseys. So in the early years of the twentieth century, bike manufacturers' names were embroidered onto some woolen jerseys, often in a rough copy of the script used in the manufacturer's logo. They were stitched by hand, using the same thick wool the jersey was made from, although in a contrasting color. This relatively crude method was improved with the introduction of lighter, thinner wool yarns to make cycling jerseys. The embroidered letters on some of those were quite exquisite.

La Française-Dunlop was one of the first professional teams, and its star rider was Maurice Garin. This is the team line up for the 1910 Paris–Roubaix.

Alcyon

1909–1955

Alcyon was a French bicycle manufacturer that also made cars and motorcycles. The word *alcyon* is French for "kingfisher," and the Alcyon team raced on kingfisher-blue bikes and wore kingfisher-blue jerseys. Four Alcyon riders—François Faber, Octave Lapize, Gustave Garrigou, and Odile Defraye—won the Tour de France from 1909 to 1912. Alcyon won again with Nicolas Frantz in 1927 and 1928, and then with Maurice De Waele in 1929. Its riders also won five Tours during the 1930s, although they represented their national team during this period, rather than Alcyon. The Alcyon pro cycling team continued until 1954, and Alcyon stayed on as a cosponsor of the Tour until 1958.

François Faber on his Alcyon bike. In 1909 the Luxembourg rider became the first foreigner to win the Tour de France. At 230 pounds (92 kilograms), he is still the heaviest to win the race.

THE TEAM

Alcyon's sponsorship of cycling began when professional road racing was a purely individual endeavor and ended long after it had become a sport in which teams work to put one of their riders into a winning position. During that time Alcyon riders won every big race there is.

The team won all five of the biggest single-day races in the sport, known as the Monuments of Cycling. They are Milan–San Remo, the Tour of Flanders, Paris–Roubaix, Liège–Bastogne–Liège, and the Tour of Lombardy, referred to nowadays simply as Il Lombardia. Alcyon won the Tour de France and Vuelta a España, four World Road Race titles, and its riders were National Champions of France, Belgium, and Luxembourg on the road and in cyclo-cross.

In total, the team won 120 world-class races, which makes it very hard to pick the top Alcyon rider. Octave Lapize has a claim, although his glittering career was cut short by the First World War, during which he was killed in fighting. The Belgian Sylvère Maes was another great Alcyon rider. The best, however, at least as far as the Tour de France is concerned, was a French rider, André Leducq.

FRANÇOIS FABER EN BELGIQUE

André Leducq won two Tours de France for the French national team, plus the Paris–Roubaix, Paris–Tours, and Critérium International for Alcyon.

Leducq won the Tour de France twice in the 1930s, although he was riding for the French national team when he did it. He also won 19 stages in the Tour, and was runner-up overall in 1928 and fourth in 1927.

THE JERSEY

Although Alcyon no longer exists as a bike brand and withdrew entirely from team sponsorship at the end of the 1950s, the kingfisher-blue jersey still exists in the pro peloton today, but only at the world championships and Olympic Games.

In 1930 the Tour de France boss Henri Desgrange declared that from then onward his race would be open to professionals, but only those professionals selected by their national federations for national, and later, regional teams. When that happened the Belgian Cycling Federation chose a black jersey with one red and one yellow band around the chest as the Belgian national team jersey.

The understated elegance of the Alcyon team jersey, designed to reflect the simple grace, but at the same time effectiveness, of the bikes Alcyon produced.

However, various Belgian racers complained that the predominantly black jersey was too hot to race in, and so in 1948 the federation changed the background of the jersey to kingfisher blue—the same as that worn by the Alcyon team. The federation added black to the yellow and red chest bands, creating a design that's still the Belgian national team jersey today. Many Belgian cycling fans think that the choice of the blue background color was due to the number of Belgian riders who had ridden in the Alcyon team, although there has been no official confirmation of this.

OCTAVE LAPIZE

In 1910, Octave Lapize won the first Tour de France stage to cross the highest passes of the Pyrenees. The stage ran for 203 miles (326 km) from Bagnères-de-Luchon to Bayonne, and the riders had to climb the Col de Peyresourde, the Col d'Aspin, the Col du Tourmalet, and the Col d'Aubisque, all of which were uncharted territories for cyclists.

It is hard to imagine now, as thousands of recreational cyclists conquer these passes each year, how much of a challenge they were in 1910, when the passes were little more than tracks used to carry goods on pack animals. The Tour de France organizers even had to pay to make the track over the Col d'Aubisque passable. While assessing the course earlier in

Octave Lapize in 1911, when he won Paris-Roubaix, Paris-Tours, Paris-Brussels, and the French national road race title.

1910, the Tour's route planner, Alphonse Steines, spent a night out on the Tourmalet after his vehicle got stuck in snow. Of course Steines, whose idea it was to include the high passes in that year's Tour, didn't tell his bosses about the incident. He just trusted there would be better weather on the day (and there was). But regardless, ahead of the competition the Tour boss, Henri Desgrange, remained worried about the riders' safety.

The Pyrenees were wild back then. Wolves and even bears lived in the mountains. Desgrange spent a nervous 24 hours until the final rider made it through. Octave Lapize was the stage winner in 14 hours 10 seconds, providing a foundation for his eventual overall victory in the race. His was an incredible achievement, in view of the fact that his bike weighed 44 pounds (20 kg) and had only two gear ratios, and also considering the poor condition of the roads and the considerable distance he had to ride.

Lapize went on to win the Paris–Roubaix and Paris–Tours classics, and three French road race titles, before the First World War broke out. He volunteered for the French Army and became one of the first fighter pilots, but was shot down near Verdun on July 14, 1917. He survived the crash, just, but died in hospital from his injuries later.

Germain Derycke in the 1954 Tour de France, riding for Belgium. He won La Flèche Wallonne and Dwars door Vlaanderen that year.

Last big win

Germain Derycke's victory in the 1955 Milan-San Remo was Alcyon's last big win. The team was called Alcyon-Dunlop then, but Alcyon had been bought by French bike giant Peugeot and the brand was slowly run down until it went out of existence. The only Alcyon bikes seen today are either in museums or have been lovingly restored by enthusiasts to ride in retro events like l'Eroica.

Thomann-Dunlop

1912—1955

Prior to the First World War, the bike company Thomann sponsored individual Tour de France riders and, in 1912, created its own eponymous team. After the war the team became Thomann-Dunlop. As professional cycling developed, the pullover came to be seen as more practical for racing than a jacket, with the design evolving from long-sleeved to short, and with pockets first at the front and then low down on the back. And in the case of professional riders, the jerseys were embroidered with the names of the team sponsors.

Marcel Bidot was a notable Thomann rider, but he became better known for his post-racing career. He was a bank clerk from Troyes, France, who turned pro in 1923, riding first for the Alcyon team, and then in 1926 and 1927 for Thomann-Dunlop. Bidot was a good pro rider, but not a great one. Instead, he made his name as the French national team manager.

He took over from his brother Jean in 1952 and presided over five French victories in the next nine years, through Louison Bobet and Jacques Anquetil. In 1962 the Tour de France went back to trade-sponsored teams, but Bidot continued to select and manage the French pro team for the World Road Race Championships.

Marcel Bidot just before the 1929 Tour de France, when he won one stage. He was also the 1929 French road race champion.

Félix Goethals of France rode for Thomann-Dunlop in 1923, when he won two stages of the Tour de France to add to his career total of seven stage victories.

Thomann-Dunlop was never a big team, and it operated at a time when for many races there was no rule on the minimum number a team could field. In the 1928 Tour de France, for example, Thomann-Dunlop only had one rider, Jan Mertens, but he still finished fourth overall, despite Alcyon-Dunlop fielding six riders and J.B. Louvet-Hutchinson ten. A Belgian born in the Antwerp suburb of Hoboken in 1904, Mertens was a good Cobbled Classics rider who also won the Tour of Flanders in 1928. It was his best year.

THE JERSEY

Thomann's company colors were orange and white, and their best race bikes were sprayed orange. So orange with a white chest band was chosen for the team colors. A white band around the middle of the jersey became a classic cycling design, as did the contrasting cuffs.

The Thomann-Dunlop team's jersey had a roll neck, a hangover from the cycling pullovers earlier racers used, but neck and side buttons were added to the design to allow some control over ventilation to cope with changes in weather conditions.

The jersey material was wool, with the heavier yarn used in the first cycling pullovers replaced by thinner wool, which led to closer knits becoming available. Close-knit wool garments were a better fit and kept their shape better, although they did tend to stretch a lot in very wet conditions.

Legnano

1922—1965

Legnano, an Italian bike brand ridden to victory by many of Italy's greatest champions, will always be associated with Alfredo Binda. While others raced in Legnano's distinctive green and red colors, Binda was the first. Legnano won six world titles, two Tours de France, and the Giro d'Italia 15 times, before it was bought by its rival Bianchi in 1968, ending its involvement as a primary team sponsor. It continued to cosponsor teams for a while, most notably the Alfa Lum-Legnano squad in 1988, whose best young rider, Maurizio Fondriest, won that year's World Road Race title in Belgium.

The timeless look of Legnano. This jersey has been reproduced recently and has proven quite popular with modern cyclists.

Alfredo Binda photographed in 1932, wearing the rainbow jersey he was awarded after securing his third and final world title.

THE RIDER

Alfredo Binda was born in 1902 in the Province of Varese, which is part of Lombardy in northern Italy. His family was very poor, so Alfredo was sent to live with his uncle, who had a plastering business in Nice. Once old enough, he served his apprenticeship there as a plasterer, and took up cycling in 1921. He won his first race soon after, and enjoyed continuing success, turning professional and joining a small French team. Lured by the big cash prizes on offer in the Tour of Lombardy, the biggest bike race in his home region, he rode from Nice to Milan in October 1924 to take part.

Binda finished fourth in the race. It was a significant achievement and announced his arrival as a serious talent. At the time, Emilio Bozzi, owner of the bike manufacturer Bozzi & Co, had just launched a new brand of bikes with Franco Tosi named after the Lombardy town of Legnano. Binda, a terrifically talented local rider, was just the man they needed to promote the brand, so Bozzi offered him a lifetime contract with his company.

The following year, Binda rode the Giro d'Italia and won it, defeating the popular old champion Costante Girardengo. Binda ultimately won the Giro five times and is still the joint record holder for victories, along with Fausto Coppi and Eddy Merckx.

Binda was also the first rider to become the official World Professional Road Race Champion, winning the title when it was inaugurated in 1927. He went on to win the World's three times, another record he still holds with Eddy Merckx, but they share this one with Belgium's Rik Van Steenbergen and the Spaniard Oscar Freire.

THE JERSEY AND THE LEGENDS

The original Legnano jersey was green with a white band around the chest, but the company quickly adopted green with red sleeves or red cuffs and a red collar— a design that is now synonymous with the Legnano name. The team jersey design remained broadly unchanged well into the 1960s, and even then the Alfa Lum-Legnano jersey of 1988 adopted the same combination of green with a red collar and cuffs. The Legnano jersey design is one of the few that spans the refinement of wool into wool-mix fibers and finally into Lycra.

The Legnano team was managed throughout its glory years by Edoardo Pavesi, whose nickname was "the lawyer." As the nickname suggests, Pavesi was a persuasive orator. He had a very keen eye for talent too. When Legnano's star, Binda, began to fade, the company's rivals Bianchi started getting the upper hand in races. It was time to find another star, and Pavesi found him in Tuscany.

In 1935, Gino Bartali won the Italian National Road Race title and the King of the Mountains title in the Giro d'Italia. He was 20 and in only his first year as a pro. Pavesi signed him for the following season, and was rewarded with wins in the Giro d'Italia and the Tour of Lombardy. It was quite a start to Bartali's career.

Gino Bartali spent his best years with Legnano, winning the Giro again in 1937 and his first Tour de France in 1938. He was an incredible climber, with an eventual seven Giro and three Tour de France King of the Mountains titles to his name, but he climbed in an odd sort of way. He almost always remained seated, and he shifted gear far more often than his competitors did, even though shifts with early derailleur gears were complicated and time-consuming. Bartali would also freewheel for a second or two every now and again when climbing. When asked why he did so, he said that easing off

Period features

Legnano is a real heritage jersey, spanning generations but preserving the DNA of the original version through its color. The classic Legnano jersey is the version from the 1940s and 1950s with a polo shirt-style buttoned collar. This also bore the name of cosponsor Pirelli, with both names embroidered in italic letters with red cotton, which exactly matched the red of the collar and sleeves.

Gino Bartali is a picture of style here, as he scales a Pyrenean climb during the 1950 Tour de France.

now and again gave his legs a break. To put that into context, the gear ratios racers had available then were much fewer and quite a bit higher than modern racers have today. Pedalling high gears slowly uphill puts a lot more strain on the legs than spinning lower gears faster. But even while Bartali was at full power, Pavesi was still looking for young talent, and in 1939 he signed a skinny, unlikely looking young man who could ride like the wind. His name was Fausto Coppi.

Coppi really was a sight when he was younger. When Bartali first saw him he said that Coppi looked "like a skinned cat." That's not a bad description, and he always remained ungainly, except when riding a bike. On two wheels, Coppi was a glory. Smoother even than Bartali, when Coppi accelerated nothing above his saddle moved; his legs would just spin faster, while his rivals tried, then failed, to maintain his pace.

Atala

Atala was one of the longest-standing sponsors in pro cycling. The winner of the first Giro d'Italia in 1909, Luigi Ganna, rode an Atala bike and was sponsored by the company, which is based in Monza near Milan and still produces bikes today. But the Atala team wasn't a constant entity in the pro peloton. Rather, the company used professional racing as a marketing method in three bursts: 1908–1925; 1946–1962; and 1982–1989.

THE GIRO LAUNCHES

Luigi Ganna had already won the 1909 Milan–San Remo when the Italian sports newspaper *La Gazzetta dello Sport* launched the inaugural Giro d'Italia on May 13. There were six stages; the first was 247 miles (397 km) and the last (and shortest), held on May 30, was 128 miles (206 km). The race went from Milan down to Rome and then up to Turin, before the final leg back to Milan. It was decided on points, with Ganna the winner. The riders were welcomed at the Milan finish by 30,000 spectators, and Ganna gave one of the most memorable quotes any Grand Tour winner has ever given. When he was asked how he felt, he told reporters, "My backside is on fire."

Love it or hate it, the 1982 Atala-Campagnolo jersey was an eye-catcher. The team name on the side panels reflects how formerly strict team jersey design rules were relaxing.

An estimated 30,000 spectators welcomed the riders to Milan at the end of the final stage of the first Giro d'Italia in 1909.

Riding for rival teams, Carlo Galetti won the Giro the following year and in 1911, after which he raced for Atala, leading a team comprising himself, Giovanni Micheletto, and Eberardo Pavesi to overall victory in the 1912 Giro d'Italia, which was run as a team race.

Vito Taccone was the star of Atala's second involvement in pro racing. A great climber, Taccone won the Tour of Lombardy and the Giro d'Italia King of the Mountains for Atala in 1961. He eventually won seven Giro stages and five King of the Mountains titles, but his career was badly affected by his inability to control his fists. He was thrown out of the 1964 Tour de France after punching the Spaniard Jesús Manzaneque. And Vittorio Adorni had to defend himself with a bike pump after outsprinting Taccone in the 1969 Italian national championships.

Trouble followed Taccone into normal life too, and, after a conviction for affray, he was sentenced to three years in prison for assault after another fight in the 1980s.

The fourth big name associated with Atala is the Swiss road sprinter Urs Freuler, who won 15 stages in the Giro and 10 world track titles. Freuler was easy to pick out in the peloton because of his black mustache and flamboyant blue and gray striped Atala jersey, which was in marked contrast to the more somber dark gray uniform of the 1920s. Through the 1940s, '50s, and '60s, the jersey was gray with dark blue chest and sleeve bands, and in the 1980s it featured alternating blue and light-gray stripes, reminiscent of the clothing you might expect jail inmates to wear. Common to all the jerseys, however, is the name Atala, embroidered in italic script, which remains the company logo today.

Sylvain Chavanel in the French National champion's jersey he won for the time trial in 2013. This was taken during a time trial stage of the 2013 Tour de France.

CHAMPIONS' JERSEYS

World and national champions race in special jerseys while they hold their titles, but only when competing in the event in which they won the title. Even when no longer world or national champions, they can carry the colors of the jersey they won on the collar and cuffs of their standard team jerseys. This chapter looks at the birth and evolution of some of the most famous champions' jerseys.

The Rainbow Jersey

1927—present day

The rainbow jersey is awarded to the winner of an official world cycling championship, and is then worn by the defending champion in that same event until a new champion is crowned. The jersey is named for the blue, red, black, yellow, and green bands around the chest, which also appear on the collars and cuffs. The rest of the jersey is white.

The rainbow jersey's design, which has remained largely unchanged over the years, is strictly controlled. This jersey was awarded to the 1985 professional world road race champion, Joop Zoetemelk.

Copyright for the rainbow bands and rainbow jersey's design is owned by cycling's governing body, the Union Cycliste Internationale (UCI). Modern rainbow jerseys have artwork depicting the format in which they are won. They are track, road time trial, mountain bike, cyclo-cross, BMX, trials, artistic cycling, and cycle ball. The only one without unique artwork is the road race rainbow jersey, which is very similar to the original rainbow jersey design.

ORIGINS

The rainbow jersey comes from colors adopted by the UCI when it formed, and they were taken from the five Olympic rings. The jersey was created by the UCI in 1927 to make the current world champion more obvious to spectators in races.

There had been world track and road race championships before that date, but 1927 saw the inaugural world professional road race championships. The road race rainbow jersey has become the most famous rainbow jersey, because men's road racing has the most followers. When people refer to "the curse of the rainbow jersey," they are referring to the series of mishaps that have befallen some winners of the world pro road race title, which is now known as the elite title.

Tom Simpson was Britain's first professional world road race champion; he was also one of the first to suffer from "the curse."

THE CURSE

A number of winners of the men's Elite World Road Race title have had a bad year while wearing the rainbow jersey, which has led to the fanciful notion that the rainbow jersey is somehow cursed. It started in 1965, when the first British winner of the elite title, Tom Simpson, broke his leg in a skiing accident early the following year and never really got back to full form that year. Simpson even crashed out of that year's Tour de France while wearing the jersey.

Things got worse when the 1970 world champion, Jean-Pierre Monseré, was killed while wearing the jersey in a small race in Belgium. His compatriot Freddy Maertens had a terrible year after taking his second world title in 1981. Whereas before his title triumph he had won around 50 races a year, in 1982 Maertens won only two.

There was also the case of Stephen Roche, who not only won the 1987 world's but also the Giro d'Italia and Tour de France that same year. But an old knee injury flared up, and his next season was a wipeout. With one or two further mishaps thrown in, Roche was never the same rider again. And the list goes on; eleven world champions since Simpson have had a bad year after they won. That's 24 percent. It makes you think, doesn't it?

Dutch rider Marianne Vos, winning the inaugural 56-mile (90-km) La Course race in 2014. This new all-female race, which is run on the same day as the Tour's final stage, is expected to significantly raise the profile of female professional cycling.

THE JERSEY

The bands represent the colors of all the countries that competed in the 1912 Olympic Games, which is when the Olympic rings on the white Olympic flag first appeared. The creator of the modern games, Baron Pierre de Coubertin, said, "The six colors [he was including the flag's white background] combined in this way reproduce the colors of every country without exception. The blue and yellow of Sweden, the blue and white of Greece, the tri-colors of France, England and America, Germany, Belgium, Italy, Hungary, the yellow and red of Spain next to the novelties of Brazil or Australia, with old Japan, and new China."

The first rainbow jersey went to the first winner of the elite world title, Alfredo Binda of Italy. Its rainbow bands were significantly wider than those on the jersey today, and it was made in the style of most cycling jerseys of the day.

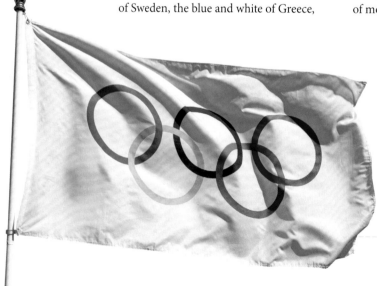

The colors of the rainbow jersey were inspired by the official symbol of the Olympic Games, the Olympic rings.

The jersey was white, made of knitted fine wool, with the bands around the chest part of the pattern and not an addition. There were rainbow bands on each sleeve, but none on the collar, which was roll-necked with side buttons reaching down and along the left shoulder, so it could be opened.

The jersey retained that style until the introduction of shirt-style buttoned collars in the 1940s. Those collars remained part of the ceremonial rainbow jersey design long after zippered collars were used for racing. By the 1970s the design had evolved into rainbow bands around the chest, collar, and cuffs, and that is how it remains today, with strict rules in place to keep it that way. The rules were made by the UCI in response to some world champions changing the design slightly, most notably the 1986 champion, Moreno Argentin of Italy. Argentin raced in a rainbow jersey on which the bands faded into one another. It wasn't nice.

Rainbow variations

The rainbow jersey for all official male or female junior, under-23, and elite world champions has a white background today. But now, as the sport has evolved, there are official world titles for para-cyclists and older racers. Para-cycling rainbow jerseys have the rainbow bands on a green background, and masters world champions get a rainbow jersey with a blue background.

Up until the 1980s, a rainbow jersey in white, with the bands going vertically down from the collar, was awarded to the winners of various European track titles. The European cycling champion's jersey is now blue, with gold stars to represent the member countries.

At the age of 22, Eddy Merckx (center) became one of the youngest ever world road race champions when he defeated Jan Janssen of the host nation, the Netherlands, and the Spaniard, Ramón Sáez, at Heerlen in 1967.

The French Champion's Jersey

1907—present

The French cycling champion's jersey is simple; it's the French national flag: the blue, white, and red Tricolor. Its design has remained unchanged since the first French professional road race champion, Gustave Garrigou, won in 1907, and so spans the gap between the wool pullover and the sleek aerodynamic racing jersey of today.

The first national champion of France, Gustave Garrigou, was a good all-round racer. As well as the 1911 Tour de France, he won the single-day Milan–San Remo in the same year.

THE FIRST WINNER

Gustave Garrigou, who was born in the Aveyron in 1884, but lived for most of his life in Paris, won the first two French professional road race titles and also the 1911 Tour de France. He was an excellent climber and a "Mr. Consistency" in races. In eight Tours de France, Garrigou won eight stages and was in the first five in 55 percent of the 117 stages he rode.

Garrigou is also famous for having had to complete one of the stages of the 1911 Tour de France in disguise. Early Tours were decided on points, and, although Garrigou got a good early lead in the race, his principal rival, Paul Duboc, had cut it down to just ten points by the time they reached the Pyrenees. However, during one of the stages there, Duboc collapsed. Although he managed to remount and finish the stage, he ended up way behind Garrigou. Suddenly the points gap was unassailable. Duboc claimed that he'd been poisoned. He'd accepted a drink from a spectator, which competitors did all the time back then, and after a while he felt terrible and had to stop riding for quite some time until he regained his senses. His fans were outraged, and they pointed the finger at Garrigou.

Jacques Anquetil, the greatest French road racer never to have won the French professional road race title.

Duboc came from Normandy, where his fanbase was located. The Tour still had to pass through Duboc's home territory, and Garrigou, who had received several death threats by then, was terrified. The race organizers took the threats seriously too, and they suggested Garrigou wear a disguise when he rode through Rouen, the city to which the threats had been traced. They even had cars drive either side of him as an extra protection. In the end, Duboc, who was cleared of involvement with the threats, finished second overall behind Garrigou, who himself had been cleared of any connection to the suspected poisoning.

THE JERSEY

Garrigou's French champion's jersey was made up of the three colors, without any contrast on the collars and cuffs. In cold conditions, he raced in a long-sleeved pullover with blue, white, and red sleeves that lined up with the colors on his body. This jersey has changed very little over the years. The only difference between Garrigou's jersey and today's French national champion's jersey, apart from its material and construction, is the addition of blue, white, and red collar and cuffs.

The Belgian National Champion's Jersey

1903—present day

The Belgian national champions' jersey is possibly the oldest unchanged jersey design in cycling. The title was inaugurated in 1894, with Léon Houa the first winner, although, due to the freedom competitors had to choose their own race clothing in those days, it is hard to pinpoint exactly when the black, yellow, and red jersey of today was first used. That said, black and white pictures of the 1903 winner, Arthur Vanderstuyft, show him wearing what could well be a black, yellow, and red horizontally banded jersey.

THREE LIONS

Like that of the French national champion, the Belgian champion's jersey consists of the national colors employed horizontally, even though the colors on the Belgian flag are, as with the French Tricolor, arranged vertically. The top third of the Belgian jersey torso is black, the middle third is yellow, and the bottom is red. Today, the sleeves are equal bands—one each of black, yellow, and red—whereas early versions of the jersey had predominantly black sleeves, with smaller yellow and red bands beneath, or yellow and red collars and cuffs.

Philippe Gilbert, Belgian road race champion in 2011 and 2016. Gilbert was also the Belgian time trial champion in 2011 and world road race champion in 2012.

The 1979 Belgian professional road champion Gery Verlinden's jersey. His team was sponsored by ice-cream manufacturer Ijsboerke and they rode Koga Miyata bikes.

Lion symbolism is strong in Belgian history and heraldry. The red section of the flag represents the lions of Hainaut, Limburg, and Luxembourg; the yellow section represents the lion of Brabant; and the black section represents the lions of Flanders and Namur. There have in the past been jerseys for regional champions, and the winner of a race that is still run today, the Championship of Flanders, receives a yellow jersey with a black lion on it, although there is no entitlement to wear the jersey in competition.

The record number of victories in the elite Belgian National Road Race Championships is held by Tom Steels, who won the title four times—in 1997, 1998, 2002, and 2004. The women's record holder is Nicole Van Den Broeck, with five titles, won between 1969 and 1977.

Belgium is and always has been a cycling stronghold, a place where being a professional cyclist is held in high esteem, so competition has always been fierce. Some Belgians have said that the Belgian national champion's jersey meant almost as much to them as winning the rainbow jersey. A look down the list of Belgian title winners certainly supports the notion that winning it is tough.

Only 19 riders have won two or more Belgian elite road race titles since 1894. The great Eddy Merckx was the world road race champion a record three times, but Belgian road race champion only once. And Erik De Vlaeminck won a record seven world cyclo-cross titles, but won the Belgian cyclo-cross title four times.

The Italian National Champion's Jersey

The Italian national champion's jersey has the same green, white, and red colors as the Italian flag. However, unlike the French and Belgian jerseys, its design has changed. The classic Italian jersey is green, white, and red, with the colors arranged horizontally, much like the French and Belgian jerseys. But it didn't start off like that, and even in recent times the jersey design has been reinterpreted by some elite road champions, who want to customize it.

THE CLASSIC JERSEY

The first Italian champion's jersey, won by Giovanni Cuniolo in 1906, was green, white, and red, with the three bands arranged vertically. The right sleeve and a right-hand section of the body were green. the middle section of the body was white, with the remainder of the body, the left sleeve, and the roll-neck collar red. Cuniolo won the title again in 1907 and 1908, and the pictures taken then of him wearing the jersey show it had vertical bands. The change in jersey design seems to have occurred soon after this. The first Italian champion to be awarded the classic jersey, with horizontal green, white and red bands, was Costante Girardengo in 1913. Girardengo also holds the record number of nine consecutive victories in this race.

The jersey design remained unchanged for quite some time, with horizontal bands on the torso, one third green at the top, one third white in the middle then red at the bottom. The sleeves had a similar green, white, and red band pattern. Then, slowly, the bottom red part grew at the expense of the other two bands, while the white band shrank the most. Despite these changes, however, the jersey was still instantly recognizable as the Italian flag.

Paolo Bettini's 2003 Italian national champion's jersey. This is the classic version of this jersey, which is instantly recognizable in the peloton.

Vincenzo Nibali's 2014 and 2015 Italian national champion's jersey is predominantly in the colors of his team sponsor Astana in this picture, but does it honor the tradition of the champion's jersey?

More recently, Italian road race champions have strayed from the classic design, wearing jerseys made up predominantly of their team colors, but with a thin band of red, white, and green around the chest. Filippo Pozzato, the 2009 champion, started the trend, and the 2014 and 2015 Italian title holder, Vincenzo Nibali, copied it.

Changing formats

The first Italian road race title, which Giovanni Cuniolo won to take the first ever Italian national champion's jersey, was decided by a specific race. However, from 1914 to 1936, 1939 to 1940, 1947 to 1949, 1951 to 1958, and 1962 to 1965 the title was decided by points awarded in anything between three and nine races, depending on the year. Aside from the championships contested during the above years, the title of Italian national champion was awarded according to the result of a single race.

The Italian Cycling Federation has been similarly adventurous with the design of the national team jersey. It used to be a deep, uniform blue, with just a tiny shield of red, white, and green on the front. It was very similar to the shirt worn by the Italian national soccer team, which is referred to as the Azzurri by fans because of its all-blue kit (*azzurro* is "sky-blue" in Italian). In the early 1990s, the Italian cycling team's jersey design changed to a much lighter blue, to which was added white, and then later red and green.

All the leaders' jerseys of
the Tour—polka-dot, green,
yellow, and white—line up in
Aix-en-Provence at the start
of stage six of the 2003
Tour de France.

THE GRAND TOUR JERSEYS

The Grand Tours are the Tour de France, Giro d'Italia, and Vuelta a España. Each one awards an overall race leader's jersey, plus jerseys for the leaders of subsidiary competitions—the King of the Mountains and the points classification. Other jerseys, which are given at each Grand Tour's discretion, include the best young rider and an intermediate sprint competition. Grand Tour jerseys are among the most famous in cycling, and this is their story.

The Yellow Jersey

1919—Present day

The Tour de France is the most famous bike race in the world. If anybody, anywhere, has heard of the concept of cycle racing, they will have heard about the Tour de France. It bestrides the sport of cycling, and, for most people, everything else sits in its shadow. And the one thing that everybody knows about the Tour de France is that the overall leader wears a yellow jersey, or *maillot jaune*, as it's called in French.

The Tour, as it's universally known in the sport, started in 1903, the brainchild of a newspaper editor and his staff. The editor was Henri Desgrange and his newspaper was called *L'Auto*. It was a sports newspaper, and in those days sports papers were the only way people could catch up on their sporting heroes. But *L'Auto* was in a circulation war with *Le Vélo*—a war that it was losing. Desgrange needed something to attract attention, and that something was the Tour de France.

A yellow jersey from the 1950s. First used to denote race leadership in the Tour de France, yellow jerseys have become a symbol for stage race leadership throughout the world.

The idea for the Tour de France came from one of Henri Desgrange's staff, but Desgrange made it work and introduced many of the current features of the race, including the yellow jersey.

The first few editions were marred by cheating and controversy, but it didn't put off the fans. They loved the Tour. It reached something deep in the French psyche—or maybe in all our psyches—because, from being a French and then a European event, the Tour de France has become the biggest annual sports event in the world.

THE JERSEY

There was no yellow jersey in the first Tour de France; in fact, its debut had to wait until the 1919 event, the first Tour after the First World War. Stage races can be confusing. The leading rider at any given point, even the stage winner, might not be leading the race overall. Desgrange's solution was to award a distinctive jersey to the leader after each stage so he could wear it the following day. It was a yellow jersey.

There are a number of stories concerning why yellow was the chosen color. The pages of *L'Auto* were yellow, so for a long time people thought that the Tour de France leader's jersey was yellow because of that. However, cycling historians have established that is not true. The yellow jersey is yellow simply because Desgrange took a long time to decide whether his idea was a good one, and by the time he made up his mind, the 1919 Tour was about to start. He needed 36 jerseys to cover all sizes for the race, and the only color any supplier had in that number was yellow, so he had no choice but to buy them. The initials HD on today's yellow jersey commemorate Henri Desgrange.

Sylvère Maes (standing) and the rest of the Belgian national team, discussing the treatment they had received from French fans during the 1937 Tour de France.

THE RIDERS

Eugène Christophe was the first rider to wear the yellow jersey, but he lost the lead in 1919 when his bike broke. A Belgian, Firmin Lambot, thus became the first yellow jersey winner. Indeed, the yellow jersey hasn't brought every rider who's worn it good luck. So far, 14 riders have dropped out of the race while wearing it. The 1936 Tour winner, a Belgian called Sylvère Maes, left the race the following year while he was leading. He was upset at the extent to which French fans were helping their countryman, Roger Lapébie, even

pushing him all the way up hills. The race judges didn't do anything about it, causing Maes to announce to journalists: "I'm not going to continue while being steadily robbed of my lead." And with that, he walked out of the race.

Most riders left because they fell ill or crashed. Perhaps the most spectacular incident involved the first Dutchman to wear the yellow jersey, Wim Van Est, who fell into a ravine. Van Est was descending the Col d'Aubisque on a Pyrenean stage in 1951 when he overshot a bend and plunged 65 feet (20 meters) straight down. Only a narrow ledge prevented him from falling farther. Van Est was hauled out by race officials and Dutch teammates, after they had knotted together all the Dutch team's spare tyres to make a rescue rope.

A spare tubular tire carried in the style Tour racers used to. Tires like this were used to lift Wim Van Est to safety after his spectacular crash in 1951.

Some riders have refused to wear the yellow jersey. Louison Bobet wouldn't wear the yellow jersey the organizers had awarded him in 1947 because he didn't like the material it was made of. The Tour had secured sponsorship from a firm called Sofil, which made fabrics using some synthetic yarn. As an experiment, the synthetic yarn was mixed with wool to make the 1947 yellow jersey, but Bobet claimed he'd ridden in a similar mix earlier in the year and it made him sweat too much. The organizers had to get some pure-wool jerseys shipped to the end of the following stage, just for Bobet.

As time passed, more manmade fibers were mixed with wool to make cycling jerseys. Wool-mix jerseys were used until the late 1980s, when wool was replaced by Lycra and similar fibers. Today, yellow jerseys are made from a variety of manmade figure-hugging materials that transport sweat away from the skin. Some materials are very light for hot stages, and others are heavier for cold or wet conditions.

Riders are awarded a yellow jersey on the podium at the end of each stage, and they used to get another one to race in during the following stage. More recently, however, the award jersey is just a ceremonial one. It has a full zipper at the back so the rider puts it on arms first and then someone zips it up for him. This is done to make the award ceremony look slick and professional.

The all-time greats

The man with the most yellow jerseys to his name is Eddy Merckx, who wore it 96 times between 1969 and 1975, on the way to winning five Tours de France. Another five-time winner, Bernard Hinault of France, is second, with 73 days in yellow. Not surprisingly, the next two places are filled by five-time winners as well: Miguel Indurain of Spain and another Frenchman, Jacques Anquetil, with 60 and 50 days respectively. Only four men have held the Tour de France yellow jersey every day from start to finish of a single Tour: Ottavio Bottecchia of Italy in 1924, the Luxembourg rider Nicolas Frantz in 1928, Romain Maes of Belgium in 1935, and Jacques Anquetil in 1961.

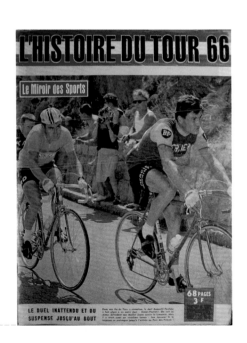

The 1966 Tour de France review edition of *Le Miroir des Sports*, showing that year's race winner, Lucien Aimar, in the yellow jersey, following Raymond Poulidor.

The Green Jersey

1953—present day

In the Tour de France, the green jersey (*le maillot vert* in French) is awarded to the cyclist who accrues the most points. Points are awarded to the first 15 cyclists across the finish line, and also to the winners of mid-stage sprints. The number of points awarded depends on the terrain of each stage, with more points awarded on flat stages than on mountain or time trial stages. That's why the green jersey is a competition for riders who sprint well, because they tend to place higher on flat stages than riders who are better climbers.

One of the Tour de France green jerseys won by three-times winner of the competition (1964, 1965, and 1967), Jan Janssen of the Netherlands.

Mario Cipollini in full yellow kit, winning stage five of the 1997 Tour de France, ahead of green jersey record holder Erik Zabel.

THE JERSEY

A competition based on points—the Grand Prix Cinquantenaire—was introduced to the Tour de France in 1953, on the Tour's 50th anniversary. It stands separate from the overall standings, which are determined by time. The first winner was a Swiss rider called Fritz Schaer, although the first rider to wear the green jersey was Wout Wagtmans of Holland. This is because Schaer won the first stage of the 1953 Tour, thus becoming Tour leader and so wearing the yellow jersey the next day. That always happens when a rider has the yellow jersey plus another. The yellow jersey takes precedence and the second rider in the other classification wears that classification's jersey.

In the first six Tour de France points competitions, the overall winner was the rider with the fewest points at the end of the race. Points were awarded accordingly, with the first rider across the line given one point, down to the fifteenth-placed rider, who was awarded fifteen points. The present system, introduced in 1959, is the reverse of this, with the most points awarded to the winner of each stage.

The competition's first sponsor was the lawn mower company La Belle Jardinière. Its company logo was predominantly green, thus prompting the Tour to award each year's points winner a green jersey. The one exception to this was in 1968, when the competition's sponsor, Sodas Sic, insisted on the jersey being red. Nowadays the green jersey rider can wear matching green shorts if he wishes, but years ago this was strictly against the rules. The man who changed that was Mario Cipollini, who by coincidence is the greatest sprinter never to have won the green jersey.

In 1997 Cipollini took the yellow jersey after winning the Tour's first road stage. Then next day he rode on a yellow bike and in yellow shorts to match the jersey, which was against Tour de France rules. The rules said the leaders of each completion in the Tour had to wear their normal team-issue shorts. Cipollini was fined, but he continued to breach the Tour's dress code at every opportunity he had. Things deteriorated to the point where the Italian wasn't invited to the race from 2000 to 2003, despite being World Road Race Champion in 2003.

At that time, though, the race director was Jean-Marie Leblanc. A former pro, Leblanc was a good director and a very fair man, but also an ardent traditionalist. He retired from the job in 2006, and was replaced for the 2007 Tour by the current director, Christian Prudhomme. Among many other innovations, Prudhomme changed the rule, allowing the jersey holders to wear matching shorts.

Triple champion

Only one man has won all three main competitions in the Tour de France—the overall, the points, and the King of the Mountains—and that was Eddy Merckx in 1969. You will see photos from that year of Merckx posing with three jerseys, a yellow, a green, and a white jersey. The white jersey was for the combined prize, which was given to the highest aggregate placing in the overall, points, and King of the Mountains competitions. There wasn't a King of the Mountains jersey in 1969. When the polka-dot jersey was introduced for the mountains leader in 1975, the white jersey was awarded to the leading young rider, and the combined jersey changed to a patchwork design made up of all the elements of the yellow, green, and polka-dot jerseys.

The combined jersey was given to the rider with the highest aggregate placings in the yellow, the polka-dot, and the green jersey competitions in the Tour de France.

Peter Sagan (center) in the 2015 Tour de France. With four straight victories in the green jersey, the Slovakian looks likely to beat Erik Zabel's record.

MOST VICTORIES

Erik Zabel of Germany has the most victories, taking the green jersey for six consecutive years from 1996 to 2001. Next are Sean Kelly of Ireland with four victories (1982, 1983, 1985, and 1989) and Peter Sagan, who also has four (2012–2015). However, at the time of writing, Sagan is only 26, and with consecutive victories up to this point in his career, he should pass Kelly and may well pass Zabel's total.

So far, Mark Cavendish is the only British winner of the green jersey. He won the competition in 2011, but he is an out and out sprinter and there is a feeling now that the distribution of points favors all-rounders who can sprint, rather than a pure sprinter in the mold of Cavendish. Looking back over the winners since 1953, however, it could be argued that this has always been the case.

The Polka-Dot Jersey

1975—present day

The leader of the King of the Mountains competition in the Tour de France wears a red and white polka-dot jersey, known in France as *le maillot à pois rouges*. However, although the first King of the Mountains award was made in 1933, a leadership jersey wasn't designated for it until 1975, and there is some debate still about its origins.

Mikel Nieve of Spain in the polka-dot jersey during the 2013 Tour de France. Britain's Chris Froome was leading the competition, but he had the yellow jersey, so the polka-dots fell to second-placed Nieve.

The most-repeated story holds that the company sponsoring the King of the Mountains competition in 1975, the French chocolate producer Chocolat Poulain, produced a bar that had a white wrapper with red dots on it. But there is very little other than anecdotal evidence to back this up. There is certainly no reference to red-spotted wrappings on the company's extensive website, and while researching this book no evidence emerged of a polka-dot wrapper. All of which makes the other story more believable.

It is claimed that the design was thought up by the then co-director of the Tour, Félix Lévitan, and that it was inspired by a similar jersey Lévitan hd seen in the Paris six-day races of the 1930s. In those days the Paris six-day was held on an indoor track called the Vélodrome d'Hiver. Lévitan had raced in his youth, and for a while he worked at the Vélodrome d'Hiver and at Paris's other famous track cycling venue, the open-air Parc des Princes.

Neither track exists now. The Vélodrome d'Hiver was demolished in 1959, and although the Parc des Princes is still a famous Paris sports stadium, the cycle track was demolished in 1967 to make way for the Boulevard Périphérique.

The first man ever to wear the polka-dot jersey was a Dutchman, Joop Zoetemelk, and the first rider to win it was Lucien Van Impe, who went on to take six Tour de France King of the Mountains titles. Van Impe is equal-second in the Tour's mountain classification victory standings, alongside Spain's Federico Bahamontes. Richard Virenque of France is in first place with eight victories.

Each jersey competition in the Tour de France is sponsored, and the sponsor's name (in this case Champion) is displayed on it.

The polka-dot jersey's design has hardly changed since 1975. The only addition is that some riders opt to wear red, or even polka-dot-patterned, shorts to match it. The current jersey sponsor, as of 2015, is the supermarket chain Carrefour. The winner in 2015 was also the yellow jersey winner, Britain's Chris Froome. The only other British winner was Robert Millar in 1984.

Richard Virenque of France, seen here in 1987, is the polka-dot jersey record holder, with eight victories in the King of the Mountains to his name.

POINTS

Points for the King of the Mountains competition are awarded at the top of each of its climbs. The climbs range from fourth category, which could be a steep hill or a short mountain climb with a relatively low gradient, to first category, which are serious mountain climbs.

There is a further category, beyond first—the Hors Catégorie, which in French means "beyond categorization." Hors Catégorie is reserved for the most famous mountain climbs of the Tour de France—

the likes of Col du Galibier, Alpe d'Huez, Col du Tourmalet, and Mont Ventoux are all Hors Catégorie climbs.

In the 2013, Tour de France riders were awarded 25 King of the Mountains points for passing first over an Hors Catégorie climb, dropping down to two points for passing in tenth place. First-category climbs offer 10 points for first and one for sixth, while one point is awarded to the first rider over a fourth-category climb.

The polka-dot jersey is one of the most recognizable and admired prizes in cycling. However, the sport's "fashionistas" are divided on the subject of polka-dot shorts.

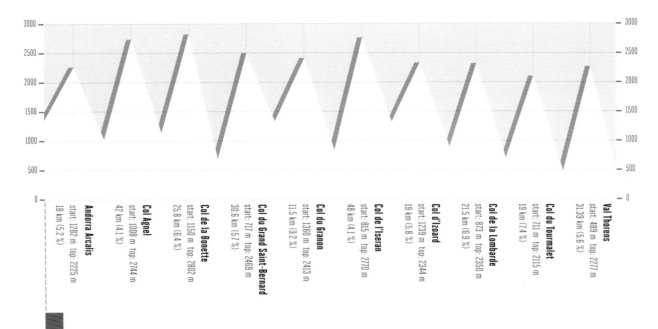

Andorra Arcalis
start: 1282 m   top: 2225 m
18 km (5.2 %)

Col Agnel
start: 1008 m   top: 2744 m
42 km (4.1 %)

Col de la Bonette
start: 1150 m   top: 2802 m
25.8 km (6.4 %)

Col du Grand Saint-Bernard
start: 717 m   top: 2469 m
30.6 km (5.7 %)

Col du Granon
start: 1360 m   top: 2413 m
11.5 km (9.2 %)

Col de l'Iseran
start: 815 m   top: 2770 m
48 km (4.1 %)

Col d'Izoard
start: 1239 m   top: 2344 m
19 km (5.8 %)

Col de la Lombarde
start: 873 m   top: 2350 m
21.5 km (6.9 %)

Col du Tourmalet
start: 711 m   top: 2115 m
19 km (7.4 %)

Val Thorens
start: 489 m   top: 2277 m
31.39 km (5.6 %)

Ten of the most challenging Hors Catégorie climbs in the Tour de France. The chart shows their start and finish heights; the gradient of each is indicated in brackets, alongside the total ascent.

Splashes of color

The Vuelta a España has always been a bit free and easy with its jersey designs. The overall leader's jersey was orange until 1941, when it changed to white. It was orange again in 1942, then, from 1945 until 1950, it was white with a horizontal red stripe. There was no Vuelta from 1951 to 1954. In 1955, when the race was resurrected, the leader's jersey was yellow. Except for 1977, when it went orange again, yellow was retained until 1992, when the color deepened to gold. In 2010 it was red, but the Vuelta overall leader's jersey has since been changed again to gold.

All very colorful, but the most garish Vuelta jersey was one given in an intermediate sprint competition, which from 2004 to 2006 was sponsored by the Spanish fishing industry and was light blue with little yellow fishes on it.

OTHER GRAND TOURS

A mountains classification was introduced in the 1933 Giro d'Italia, although there was no leader's jersey until 1974. Plain green was the chosen color, and this was retained until 2012, when a new sponsor of the mountains classification, Banca Mediolanum, wanted a blue jersey for the duration of their sponsorship, which, at the time of writing, runs until the end of 2016.

The Vuelta a España has had a number of mountains leaders' jerseys. For many years it was green, but in 1986 there was a red jersey with white polka dots, and in 1989, when the mountains classification was sponsored by Café de Colombia, the leader's jersey was white with a brown coffee-bean pattern. More recently the Vuelta's mountains jersey has been white with large blue polka dots.

The Pink Jersey

The pink jersey, or *maglia rosa* in Italian, denotes the leader of the Giro d'Italia. It first appeared in the 1931 edition of Italy's Grand Tour, and is pink because the pages of the race sponsor, the sports newspaper *La Gazzetta dello Sport*, are pink. As with the yellow jersey, its color has never changed, although its design has, especially in recent years.

The first Giro d'Italia was in 1909. Like the Tour de France, the Giro was born out of a war between two newspapers, *Corriere della Sera* and *La Gazzetta dello Sport*. Both wanted to put on a race that mimicked the Tour de France, and it was *La Gazzetta*, with prior experience of organizing bike races, that got its act together more quickly. The first Giro d'Italia began on May 13, 1909, and ended on May 30. There were six stages across a total distance of 1521 miles (2447.9 km).

The race was decided on points, which were awarded according to the finish order of every stage. This was to avoid problems that had beset the 1904 Tour de France, when partisan supporters stopped and held back riders, to allow their favorite riders to gain time. Running the race on points removed the incentive for spectators to get involved in that way. But it also resulted in the eventual winner, Luigi Ganna, not being the quickest over the entire course. If the 1909 race had been decided on time, the third-placed rider, Giovanni Rossignoli, would have won by quite a margin.

A 1914 issue of *La Gazzetta dello Sport*, showing the pink pages that inspired the *maglia rosa*, the pink jersey of the Giro d'Italia.

One of the pink jerseys worn by Eddy Merckx when leading the Giro d'Italia during the 1970s. This jersey was sponsored by the Clément tire company.

THE JERSEY

The first *maglia rosa*, won by the Italian racer Francesco Camusso in 1931, was entirely pink and made from wool, with a roll-neck collar and front pockets for holding food. A gray shield was sewn in the middle of the chest, bearing the symbol of the Italian fascists. It was on the jersey by the ruling Fascist Party's decree.

The jersey remained solid pink for the rest of the 20th century, but since 2000 there have been slight changes to the design. The 2006 jersey, for example, had a bike motif picked out in darker pink. Then in 2009, to celebrate the Giro's centenary, the jersey's collar and side panels were edged with the green, white, and red colors of the Italian flag.

That jersey was designed by Dolce and Gabbana, and the trend for guest fashion designers continued with Paul Smith designing the 2013 pink jersey. He called his creation the *maglia rosa passione*. Then in 2014, when the race started in Belfast, all the Giro d'Italia classification jerseys were created by the Irish designer Fergus Niland, on behalf of the Italian cycling clothing company Santini. The jersey featured stylized shamrock and tweed motifs, and bore the legend "Giro Fights for Oxfam," as well as the jersey sponsor Balocco's name.

THE RIDERS

The man with the most days in the pink jersey is that holder of so many cycling records, Eddy Merckx. He won the Giro five times, amassing a total of 77 days in the pink jersey. Nearest to him is Alfredo Binda, with 65 days in the lead for five victories, although his success came between 1925 and 1933, meaning much of it predates the pink jersey.

If anything though, Binda was more dominant than Merckx. In 1927, he won 12 of the 15 stages that made up the race, and in 1929 he won eight consecutive stages. But this was an age of heroism in cycling, and Binda was an excellent tactical rider who never wasted effort. His way of winning became so ruthlessly efficient that the Giro organizers thought he was making the race boring. In 1930, they paid him 22,000 lire not to ride the Giro.

Only one man has won all three main jerseys in the Giro d'Italia, and you won't be surprised to hear that it was Eddy Merckx. He won the overall, points, and mountains in the 1968 Giro, which was his first Grand Tour victory. However, the following year Merckx was thrown off the Giro while in the pink jersey due to a positive dope test. He protested his innocence, claiming his sample had been tampered with. He went to great lengths to prove it too, and the suspension he was given was lifted on a balance of probabilities basis, so Merckx could ride the 1969 Tour de France.

Alfredo Binda, the first big star of the Giro d'Italia. This photograph was taken while he was competing in an indoor six-day race.

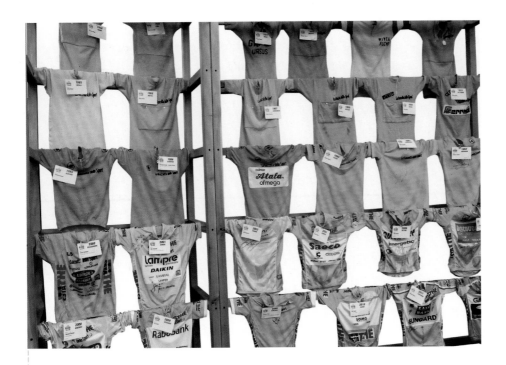

The collection of pink jerseys held in the Cycling Museum at the top of the Madonna del Ghisallo climb near Como in northern Italy. They show the way the design has changed and evolved over time.

Cycling's master tailor

The first Giro d'Italia's pink jerseys were made by the pioneer of Italian cycling clothing, Vittore Gianni. He was a tailor who founded a business in Milan in 1896, with the soccer teams AC Milan and Juventus, and the Milan Ballet, among his regular clients. He started making cycling clothing in 1910, and was soon making clothing for Alfredo Binda and other champions.

In 1935, Vittore Gianni was joined by Armando Castelli, who bought the business from Vittore in 1939. Retaining the Gianni brand name, Castelli continued making jerseys and shorts out of fine merino wool for the likes of Fausto Coppi, Gino Bartali, and Rik Van Looy, as well as supplying 12 professional teams. In 1974, Armando's son, Maurizio, took over the business and changed its name to Castelli, after which the company took over the manufacture of the pink jersey for the Giro d'Italia. However, in the last few years, the jerseys have been supplied by another Italian manufacturer, Santini. Made from lightweight polyester fabric, with some inserts on back and pockets in Cyber Rider fabric, the modern pink jersey's finish is designed to resemble the rough look of an asphalt road surface. The jersey is finished with elasticated cuffs and an elasticated band around the bottom, with an internal anti-sliding silicon grip, to make it more aerodynamic.

Riders at the start of a
stage in the 1929 Tour de
France, the last one open
to trade-sponsored teams.
The following year, all these
jerseys would be replaced by
those of the riders' nations.

1920s TEAM JERSEYS

By the mid-1920s, cycling jerseys were tailored much more to their task. Rear pockets, in addition to those on the front, appeared toward the end of the decade. Also, while some pro riders had their sponsors' names on their jerseys before the 1920s, lettering became a universal feature during this decade. This was also the time when riders began racing as teams, with designated leaders and helpers.

Automoto-Hutchinson

1920–1929

Although cycling authorities during the 1920s permitted only bike manufacturers to be a team's headline sponsor, they did allow bicycle tire manufacturers as junior sponsors. Bike manufacturer Automoto was joined by Hutchinson, a well-known French tire brand, to form a team that produced the winning riders of the 1923, 1924, and 1925 Tours de France.

Automoto was founded in 1900 in Paris and made bikes, then cyclomoteurs (mopeds). It became part of the Peugeot group in 1930 and ceased trading in 1963. Automoto's race bikes were produced in two colors, blue and purple, which is why the team jersey swapped from one color to the other every year.

The first stars of the team were the Pélissier brothers, Francis and Henri, with the latter winning the 1923 Tour de France for Automoto-Hutchinson. A third Pélissier, the youngest brother Charles, was also part of the team, but enjoyed his best years in another jersey. The other big name was Ottavio Bottecchia.

Automoto sold bikes in Italy, so the team enlisted a number of Italian racers to ride the 1923 Tour de France, but only Bottecchia turned up. He proved to be a big hit. Armed with one French phrase, "No bananas, lots of coffee, thank you," which he used to pick up his rations, Bottecchia was so strong in 1923 that Henri Pélissier, the race winner, correctly predicted he would win in 1924. Bottecchia was the first Italian to win the Tour de France.

The middle Pélissier brother, Francis. During the First World War, like many Tour de France riders, he served in the French armed forces.

Francis Pélissier leading in the 1919 Paris–Roubaix, a race where the normally bad roads had been further decimated by the First World War.

THE JERSEY

By the mid-1920s, cycling jerseys were getting quite refined. Gone were the heavy-knit pullovers. Instead, top racers wore jerseys made from fine wool, very often the finest merino, which were a good fit and kept their shape.

This Automoto-Hutchinson jersey clearly shows the deep front chest pockets cycling jerseys had in the 1920s.

Riders in big international road races, such as the Tour de France, preferred long-sleeved jerseys, which gave some protection against the cold during early-morning starts, which were necessary for the longest stages. They could have worn extra jerseys, but the rules forbade them from discarding excess clothing, meaning they would have had to carry unwanted garments for the duration of the stage. In 1924, this caused a massive argument between Automoto's Henri Pélissier and the Tour boss, Henri Desgrange.

Desgrange discovered that Pélissier had ditched a jersey during a stage, so he gave the volatile Frenchman a time penalty. Pélissier's anger was exacerbated when his clothing was examined on two separate occasions by race officials. Pélissier and his brother Francis left the race and gave a hastily convened interview to a journalist, Albert Londres. That was when they blew the lid on the drugs riders used in the Tour then to help them get through the race.

One of the first pictures to appear of Bottecchia, taken just before the 1923 Tour de France.

OTTAVIO BOTTECCHIA

Bottecchia had not ridden a bike before he joined the army, becoming a cycle messenger in the elite Bersaglieri light infantry unit. He proved to be a good cyclist, and, after he was discharged, Bottecchia decided to try to make money as a professional racer.

He turned professional after one year with the amateurs. As an independent rider, he won several good races, and in 1923 finished 11th overall in the Giro d'Italia. That brought the invitation from Automoto-Hutchinson to take part in the Tour de France.

Bottecchia cut an unlikely figure. Short, incredibly skinny, and with skin the color of tanned leather, his impish, somewhat wizened face was scored by deep lines and framed by prominent ears. None of which mattered in the slightest, because he really could ride a bike.

Early in the 1923 Tour de France, Bottecchia won a stage and took the yellow jersey, after which he ably supported Henri Pélissier. Automoto-Hutchinson immediately signed him up for the following year with the promise of higher pay.

Bottecchia's demise

On June 3, 1927, Bottecchia was found sprawled out by the roadside, some distance from his bike, with his skull fractured and other broken bones. There were no marks on the road or on his bike to indicate a fall, and he died from his injuries a few days later.

There are many theories as to the cause of Bottecchia's death. He wasn't popular with the ruling Fascist Party, and years later an Italian made a deathbed confession in New York, saying he had killed Bottecchia for the Mafia. The claim remains unsubstantiated, and the mystery of the little Italian's death persists.

Bottecchia was almost unchallenged in the 1924 Tour de France. He won the first stage, 237 miles (381 km) from Paris to Le Havre, and then, with the yellow jersey on his back, he won two more to take the race overall. He was so thrilled to win, he wore his final yellow jersey on the train all the way back home to Milan, singing snatches of opera along the way.

He often sang opera on the bike too, and he had plenty of time to do it when he won the 1925 Tour, with a very talented Belgian, Lucien Buysse, helping him. By then, the term "domestique" was well used in pro cycling. It had been a term of approbation coined by Henri Desgrange in 1911, when he wrote about Maurice Brocco. After giving up all hope of winning the overall

competition himself, Brocco made it known that he would help any contender for a price. Although this development outraged Desgrange's Corinthian sensibilities, the Tour manager was helpless to prevent the practice from spreading, especially as teams became more organized.

Cycling success appeared easy for Bottecchia, although, such were the distances covered during races in the 1920s, it was anything but. However, after dropping out of the 1926 Tour during an exceptionally demanding stage in the Pyrenees that was held despite a thunderstorm, Bottecchia was never the same again. He tried for years to come back, but his health was fragile and he couldn't regain his strength.

Lucien Buysse leading his teammate Bottecchia on the final stage of the 1925 Tour de France, which Bottecchia won, with Buysse second.

Alleluia-Wolber

1916–1955

The Alleluia-Wolber team operated for almost 40 years and employed a number of very good riders. One rider, the youngest of the Pélissier brothers, Charles, was the first sprinter of the Tour de France. He still shares the record of eight stage wins in one Tour (in 1930), along with the Belgians Eddy Merckx and Freddy Maertens. He won another five in 1931, finishing with a career total of 16.

Cycles Alleluia was a Paris bike manufacturer with a huge range of bikes, producing everything from heavy-duty delivery bikes to lightweight racers. The team's jerseys went through several changes, starting with a design of light blue, with a tartan-patterned chest band, on which a patch bearing the trademark Alleluia ringing bell was sewn. The next generation of Alleluia jerseys were blue, with a white chest band and, later on, it changed to green, with a red chest band. Early jerseys bore the gothic lettering of the Alleluia name, which was also featured on the bikes. By the mid-1920s, some cycling jerseys were being made with rear pockets.

Alleluia was probably most famous for making delivery bikes, which were used extensively in Paris. Alleluia bikes often featured in the annual Critérium des Porteurs de Journaux in Paris, a race for newspaper delivery bikes. It should be noted that the race was for delivery bikes rather than people delivering the newspapers, given that manufacturers often fielded suspiciously old-looking delivery boys. Some of them must have been good amateur racers; the 1933 winner, for example, averaged a speed of over 23 miles per hour (37 kph) on cobbled streets, riding a heavy bike loaded with newspapers.

Another remarkable rider in the Alleluia-Wolber jersey was Hubert, later Sir Hubert, Opperman. Known in Australian cycling circles as "Oppy," Hubert Ferdinand Opperman was an Australian racer who traveled to Europe in April 1928, after winning almost every race there was to win at home. He was accompanied by two other Australians and a New Zealander, and their intention was to enter the Tour de France.

Hubert Opperman receives flowers and a kiss after winning a race in France in 1928.

Competitors in the annual newspaper delivery boys' race in Paris. The accompanying vehicles and determined looks on the faces of competitors show it was quite a serious affair.

Opperman won several big races, including the prized Bol d'Or 24-hour race, and finished a very creditable 18th overall in the 1928 Tour de France for the Ravat-Wolber-Dunlop team. He returned to Europe in 1931 and rode for Alleluia, for whom he won Paris–Brest–Paris. He also rode the Tour de France in 1931 for the joint Australian–Swiss team (the Tour that year was contested by national teams), finishing 12th overall. Afterward, he returned to Australia and became a politician. In 1955, he was appointed the Minister for Transport, and between 1963 and 1966 he served as Minister for Immigration.

The great French rider Antonin Magne started his professional racing career with Alleluia-Wolber in 1926. He progressed steadily, achieving three top-ten finishes in the Tour de France, before leaving the team in 1930. Magne went on to win two Tours, and in the second chapter of his cycling life became one of the most famous team managers.

Dilecta-Wolber

1922-1957

Dilecta-Wolber was good at finding talent, but not good at keeping it. Francis and Charles Pélissier started their careers with the team, but had their best victories elsewhere. Maybe that is why the team turned to Belgium after the 1920s, recruiting many of its riders there. The move certainly brought the team more success, especially in the single-day Classics races.

BELOVED BIKES

Dilecta bikes was founded in 1913 by Albert Chichery in Le Blanc in the Indre department of France. Chichery made a fortune during the First World War and invested a lot of money in improving his factory's production capacity. He entered politics and became the Deputy for l'Indre, and later Minister of Commerce and Industry in the Vichy Government during the Second World War. He was assassinated by the French Resistance on August 15, 1944.

Dilecta is from the Latin for "beloved." The company's first emblem had the words Dilecta and Le Blanc either side of Chichery's initials, but it was soon changed to a silhouette of a young woman inside a star. The emblem was sewn onto the first Dilecta-Wolber team jerseys, which were orange, with French Tricolor bands on the sleeves. The team also raced in orange and blue quartered caps, or casquettes, as they are known in cycling.

The Pélissier brothers (left to right): Charles, Francis, and Henri, after the 1926 Critérium des As held in Paris.

Ferdinand Le Drogo finishes first on stage three of the 1927 Tour de France, beating Marcel Huot and Francis Pélissier.

Dilecta's first star rider was Ferdinand Le Drogo, who won the French professional road race title in 1927 and 1928. Charles Pélissier won the 1928 French cyclo-cross title for the team, before moving to a rival team.

By 1930, Dilecta was employing more Belgian racers, but some years earlier the team jersey started switching between two designs. The first was a blue upper and a yellow lower half, with blue sleeves and yellow cuffs. And the second had yellow upper and blue lower halves. It had front pockets and a turtle-neck collar, opened with buttons along the left collarbone area.

DON FREDO

Dilecta's top riders during the 1930s were Romain Gijssels, who won Paris–Roubaix and Bordeaux–Paris in 1932, and Frans Bonduel, who achieved several top-ten placings in the Tour de France. And in 1931 the team signed up a rider who could have been a huge international star.

His name was Fred Hamerlinck, and he came from Ghent in Belgium. He was the star of a special kind of race, which is still staged in Flanders, called the *kermesse*. When Hamerlinck raced, every town, village, and city suburb had a kermesse race as part of the annual fair.

The riders raced around street circuits 5–6 miles (8–10 km) in length, completing 15–20 laps, for big cash prizes. Hamerlinck, who his fans called Don Fredo, once won five of these hotly contested races in one week, and ended his career winning a total of 493 races.

Don Fredo won two stages of the 1931 Tour de France, but it cost him money. Spending three weeks racing around France netted him far less cash than three weeks of kermesses would have. Hamerlinck continued racing for Dilecta (the Belgian market was important for them) but he never rode the Tour de France again.

J.B. Louvet

1914—1937

Founded in 1903 in Puteaux, then a separate town but now a suburb of Paris, the J.B. Louvet bike manufacturing company had a flair for marketing. Not only did it start sponsoring individual racers in 1904 and a team from 1914, J.B. Louvet commissioned some outstanding posters of the kind bike manufacturers used to advertise their goods in those days. Many of them were produced by an artist who signed the posters as MICH. His real name was Michel Libiaux, and his work was much in demand toward the end of an era in which painted poster adverts employed several great artists, including Henri de Toulouse-Lautrec.

One of Michel Libiaux's posters, painted for J.B. Louvet. His "Mich" trademark signature can be seen in black, close to the lower rungs of the step-ladder.

Eugène Christophe, the first rider to wear the yellow jersey, and an early innovator in professional cycling.

THE PARROTS

The J.B. Louvet race bikes were painted green and had red handlebar tape. The team's matching green and red jerseys earned it the nickname "The Parrots" from cycling fans. In 1921, Francis and Henri Pélissier, though up against better resourced teams with more riders, scored a one–two finish to take Paris–Roubaix for J.B. Louvet.

J.B. Louvet's 1922 jersey was dark green with a red chest band. The short-sleeved jerseys had red cuffs, while the long-sleeved variant had a red band halfway down each arm, which aligned with the chest band when the riders stood for photographers. The J.B. Louvet name was embroidered on the front in white across two lines—"J.B." at the top and "Louvet" beneath, all in block capitals. There was one front pocket, and a buttoned roll neck for ventilation. Later jerseys had rear pockets as well.

Eugène Christophe joined J.B. Louvet in 1925, toward the end of this career, and became one of its most famous racers. Christophe was the first man to wear the yellow jersey in the Tour de France, but in a career dogged by bad luck, he was one of the best racers never to have won the Tour.

Christophe was a great innovator who thought about his cycling and tried to improve his bikes, making them more dependable and efficient. He is credited with inventing the toe clip, a piece of sprung steel that bolted to a bike's pedals and went over the rider's foot. Toe clips vastly improved pedaling efficiency, especially when combined with toe straps (which thread through the pedal and toe clip at right angles to the toe clip), by ensuring a rider's foot was held securely in place. Christophe sold his design to Poutrait-Morin (later Zéfal) in 1925, and Christophe-branded toe clips were bought by racing cyclists right up until clipless pedals took over in the early 1990s.

Coincidentally, another member of the 1925 J.B. Louvet team, Hector Martin, was an innovator and proved to be a great businessman. He came from Roeselare, which is the center of the Belgian shoe manufacturing industry. After he stopped racing, Martin launched his own brand of fine leather cycling shoes, which established themselves as industry leaders.

Elvish-Wolber

1928–1933

Elvish-Wolber was created in 1928 to back one man, Victor Fontan, in the Tour de France. Fontan came from Pau, the town at the foot of the Pyrenees where the bicycle company Elvish was based. Unfortunately for Fontan, the riders hired to back him weren't strong, and in the 1928 Tour every stage was run as a team time trial. It wasn't a very fair way of deciding the Tour de France, and it changed for 1929.

Victor Fontan in 1929; has any Tour de France winner looked more French than this?

UNIFORM STYLE

The Elvish-Wolber jersey was bright green, with an orange chest band and orange mid-sleeve bands. This was a standard pattern for team jerseys by the late 1920s, and the Elvish-Wolber jersey was similar to the J.B. Louvet design. This could indicate they were made by the same manufacturer, possibly Bovis of Paris, who made a lot of later French team jerseys.

In 1929, team time trials were dropped from all but three stages, and Fontan took the yellow jersey on stage seven to Bordeaux. Or at least he shared it. For the first time in history, three riders—Nicolas Frantz, André Leducq, and Fontan—had exactly the same time, so they shared the lead. They lost it next day to the Belgian Gaston Rebry, but Fontan took it back after the following stage. This time he led on his own, completing a terrific ride through the Pyrenees, in which he finished second but opened up a 9-minute lead.

The Italian rider Giusto Cerutti trying to finish a stage of the 1928 Tour de France after his bike was irreparably damaged in a crash.

However, disaster soon followed. Fontan had only ridden 4 miles (7 km) of the subsequent 200-mile (323-km) stage when he crashed badly, breaking the forks of his bike. In 1929, the Tour de France rules said that Fontan could use a replacement bike, but only after he had shown a race judge that it was impossible to continue on the bike he'd started with. But it was early in the race, and all the judges had gone ahead of Fontan. The truck with the spare bikes had gone ahead too.

Fontan was left to walk to the next village, where he went house to house, asking if someone would lend him a bike. They eventually did, and Fontan set off after the Tour, with his broken bike tied to his back. He had to take it with him, because if he couldn't prove it was broken he would be disqualified.

It was too much, though. Fontan gave up after a hopeless chase, sat down by the fountain in St. Gaudens, and cried his eyes out. This was a historic moment. The 1929 Tour de France was the first to be covered by radio, and the radio team of Jean Antoine and Alex Virot found Fontan in St Gaudens, who then gave them an emotional interview. This resulted in an outcry in the press, asking if it was right that a man should lose the race because of a broken bike. Next year the Tour de France director, Henri Desgrange, changed the rules, allowing teams to swap bikes. From then on, if the leader got into trouble, a teammate could give him his bike.

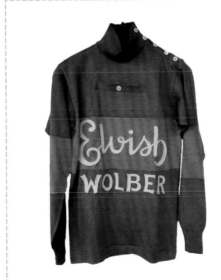

This Elvish-Wolber jersey from 1928 is well designed, with a long run of shoulder buttons and tightly knitted cuffs— two features that would have improved comfort.

A French national team lines
up before a race dressed in
the 2016 design of the French
national team jersey.

NATIONAL TEAM JERSEYS

The 1930s saw the Tour de France switch from having trade-sponsored teams to inviting professional riders to represent their nations. This was, understandably, very unpopular with the trade teams, but it did give rise to national team jerseys, which are still worn by pro racers in the world championships each year. And as you will see, some of the jersey designs have changed very little.

The French National Team Jersey

1930—present day

Five national teams were invited to take part in the 1930 Tour de France—France, Belgium, Italy, Germany, and Spain. Each team contained eight riders, all wearing identical jerseys incorporating the colors of their national flag. Today, professional riders will compete in their national colors only during the world championships and Olympic Games. Of those original jerseys worn in the 1930 Tour, the French jersey has changed the least.

ORIGINS

The impetus behind the change came from the race director, Henri Desgrange, who thought that the trade-sponsored pro teams had become so professional that they displayed a somewhat cynical attitude to the race. Desgrange wanted to stop that, so in 1930 the teams Desgrange invited took part at the Tour's expense. The race even provided the team riders with identical bikes, painted yellow and unbranded, and said they had to ride them. The rest of the field was made up of riders called touriste-routiers. They supplied their own clothing and bikes, and they made their own arrangements for accommodation.

The French jersey was in the red, white, and blue colors of the French flag, the Tricolor, but unlike the French national champion's jersey, which is a straight copy of the flag, the French team jersey was predominantly blue with a white and red chest band. And 86 years later, that is how the French national team jersey still looks. It is one of the most enduring jersey designs of all, almost on a par with the rainbow, yellow, and pink jerseys in terms of continuity.

THE 1930 TOUR DE FRANCE

The revamped Tour was dominated by France. It was 3011 miles (4818 km) long and divided into 21 stages, with five rest days, so it lasted almost a month. Charles Pélissier of the French national team won the first stage in a two-man sprint alongside Alfredo Binda of Italy—a finale that set the pattern for the rest of race. Pélissier was the first great sprinter of cycling, and he won a total of eight stages in 1930—a record he shares with Freddy Maertens and Eddy Merckx of Belgium.

Italy took the yellow jersey through their national champion, Learco Guerra, on stage two, but André Leducq of France took over in the Pyrenees on stage nine. But then Leducq crashed badly in the Alps. It happened on the long descent of the Col du Galibier's north side, and Leducq was knocked unconscious.

It took 15 minutes for him to fully gain his senses, by which time almost the whole French team had stopped to help its stricken leader. They got him going again, but it was a struggle. Then came the short climb up the Col du Télégraphe, and Leducq crashed again when his pedal broke, this time making a terrible mess of his knee.

L'ILLUSTRÉ
DU PETIT JOURNAL
TOUS LES DIMANCHES · ET SON SUPPLÉMENT AGRICOLE · GRAND HEBDOMADAIRE POUR TOUS · 50c. · 9-7-33

UNE ÉTAPE DU TOUR DE FRANCE

Cette année, les départs sont donnés aux heures qui permettent au public de nos provinces d'y assister. Scènes pittoresques. Avant l'étape, les coureurs se rafraîchissent. Antonin Magne signe la carte que lui tend une admiratrice. Leducq est à ses côtés. Les équipes sont prêtes. Tous vont s'élancer à la conquête du "Tour".

A 1933 French magazine cover showing the French national team engaging with fans outside a café before the start of a stage in the Tour de France. The Belgian and Italian teams can be seen in the background.

Leducq thought his knee was broken, and sat nursing it with his back against a low wall. But then his teammate, Marcel Bidot, grabbed the foot of his affected leg and pushed it upwards to bend his knee, and said, "If it was broken you couldn't do that. Now stop blubbering, the yellow jersey never gives up. Look, the whole team has stopped to help you." And Leducq remounted his bike, and the French team paced him to the stage finish in Grenoble, catching his rivals in the process, and saving the Tour de France for him. In Paris, Leducq was 14 minutes ahead of Guerra, sealing the first of two Tour de France victories in his career, and the first of five consecutive Tour victories for the all-powerful French national team.

THE JERSEY

In 1930 and 1931 the French team jersey was long-sleeved, and predominantly light blue, with white and red bands around each elbow, as well as around the chest. In 1932, short-sleeved jerseys were introduced, and in 1934 they had a darker blue base color, although retaining the white and red bands. They also had a red, white, and blue band around the collar and cuffs.

That pattern was preserved through the 1940s, with the addition of the crest of the governing body of French cycling, the FFC, stitched to the center of the chest. Then in the 1950s and early '60s, the jersey changed in response to fashion, with the addition of button-up polo-shirt collars. By the '60s, the sleeves were white above red, with no contrasting cuff. From 1960 to 1962 the sleeve pattern was inconsistent. Some jerseys had blue (uppermost), then white and red bands. Some were just white above red. Neither pattern had contrasting cuffs.

The Tour de France went back to trade-sponsored teams in 1962, but the Tour organizers reintroduced national teams for the 1967 and 1968 Tours. In those Tours the French team wore the national jersey once more, but 1968 was the final year for national teams in the Tour de France. Trade-sponsored teams came back in 1969, and the Tour has been contested by the best of those teams ever since.

The 1932 French Tour de France team. From left to right: André Leducq, Albert Barthélémy, Julien Momeau, Louis Peglion, Marcel Bidot, Maurice Archambaud, Georges Speicher, and Roger Lapébie.

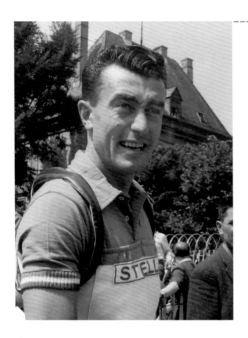

Louison Bobet, one of the most successful men ever to wear the French team jersey.

Les bleus

Les bleus is the name given to the French team in the Tour, and some great riders have worn in the national jersey. Louison Bobet won three consecutive Tours (1953–1955) in the French national jersey, the first rider ever to achieve that feat. Another ground-breaker for the French team was Jacques Anquetil, who won two Tours (1957 and 1961) as part of the team. He went on to record five Tour wins—the first time this had been achieved—and he still holds the joint record for Tour wins.

Eight Frenchmen have won the world professional road race title in the national team jersey, including Antonin Magne in 1936, Louison Bobet in 1954, and Bernard Hinault in 1980. And because the French national team jersey has stayed unchanged for so long, the great Jeannie Longo won five road race and four time trial world titles, plus one Olympic road race title, in a jersey design not so different from that worn by the French team in the 1930 Tour de France. And something very similar is still worn by French riders in the world championships and Olympic Games in all cycling disciplines today.

Jeannie Longo, definitely the most successful French woman for the national team, with one Olympic gold medal, five world titles, and the World Hour Record.

The Italian Tour de France Team Jersey

1930–1968

Every national team jersey in the 1930 Tour de France had the same basic design, with only the colors varying. Unlike the French, however, the Italian team used a different jersey in world championships and Olympic Games from that used in the Tour de France. In those races, they used the famous "Azzurri," the blue color made famous by the Italian national soccer team. Today, the Italian national cycling team jersey is still predominantly blue, although not the Azzurri blue that looked so special.

Totally understated, totally cool; the simple Azzurri jersey of the Italian national team.

THE LOCOMOTIVE

The star of the 1930 Italian Tour de France team was Learco Guerra, a powerful racer who was called the "human locomotive" by his legion of fans. Guerra, who came from Lombardy, earned the moniker thanks to the way he raced. Simply put, he went to the front of the peloton and rode as hard as he could. He wasn't a gifted climber, but his strength was legendary. He set such a hard pace over flat or rolling terrain that he slowly burned the other riders off his wheel. Then, while they chased as a group, taking it in turns to set the pace, Guerra would move ever farther away from them.

Guerra won two stages in this way in the 1930 Tour de France, and eventually finished second overall. But he performed best in single-day races, which suited his style. His victory in the 1930 Italian national road race championship was the first of five consecutive national titles, and he won the world road race championships in 1931. He also won Milan–San Remo in 1933 and Il

Guerra leads on the
Col du Tourmalet on stage
9 of the 1930 Tour de France.
The stage went from Pau
to Bagnères-de-Luchon.

Lombardia (the Tour of Lombardy) in 1934. Guerra eventually won seven Tour de France stages in his career, and 31 stages in the Giro d'Italia, including an incredible ten in 1934, when he won the race overall. That was his only Grand Tour victory.

Guerra's prodigious strength was said to come from his first job, which involved riding a tandem to a sand quarry, filling two huge saddle bags located where the rear rider would sit, then pedaling the load of sand to building sites. He repeated the

task all day long, six days a week. It's no surprise that when Guerra started racing, he started winning.

But Italy was going through a politically torrid time in the 1930s, and although he had no interest, Guerra found that one of the conditions for his gaining a place in a pro team was membership of the Fascist Party. Then, with his success, he became a favorite of the party leader, Benito Mussolini. His achievements were politicized, becoming propaganda tools for Mussolini's Fascists to exploit.

THE JERSEY

In a similar design to the French, the Italian Tour de France team jersey was green, with a white and red band around the chest. The 1930 jersey was long-sleeved, with a white band around the elbow as well. From 1931, the riders wore short-sleeved jerseys, with the same chest bands, plus white and red collars and cuffs. From the late 1940s to the early '60s, the jerseys had polo-shirt collars. The Italian Tour de France jersey stopped being used in 1968, the year of the last Tour to be operated according to the national team format. In the world championships and Olympic Games, Italian riders continued wearing the all-blue jerseys—a single block of the most perfect shade of blue, with no contrasting collars or cuffs, and just a small patch of the Italian flag sewn on the chest. It was a design classic.

As other federations had, the Italian Cycling Federation decided to modernize its jersey. They added color, contrasts, and the name "Italia." It didn't need it; perfect jersey designs are best left untouched. So instead of being the ultimate in cycling cool, the Italian national jersey today looks like it was designed by committee, which it probably was.

Gino Bartali in the 1950 Tour de France. The Italian team jersey for the Tour was still green, with a red and a white chest-band, but had acquired a polo shirt-style collar.

Members of the Italian women's team in the predominantly blue jerseys the national team has worn in the world championships.

Fausto Coppi taking a lap of honor in the yellow jersey of the 1952 Tour de France.

Coppi and Bartali

The period between the late 1930s and the early 1950s was a golden era for Italy in the Tour de France, and in cycling as a whole. It was the era of Coppi and Bartali. Gino Bartali was a great champion. He won the 1938 and 1948 Tours de France, and he could have won more, had the Second World War not interrupted the competition. But Fausto Coppi was *Il Campionissimo*, the Champion of Champions. Alongside Eddy Merckx, he is a contender for the crown of greatest cyclist there has ever been. Coppi won two Tours, in 1949 and 1952, both of them as leader of the Italian national team.

Coppi and Bartali were both affected by the war. Coppi was conscripted into the Italian Army and captured by the allies, spending time as a prisoner of war, while Bartali was engaged in heroic, and extremely dangerous, undercover work. He was part of the Assisi Line that helped smuggle Jews out of Italy, right under the noses of the Italian Fascist and German Nazi authorities.

The Belgian Tour de France Team Jersey

1930—1968

It was a Belgian who finally brought about the end of national teams in the Tour de France. Eddy Merckx was only 23 in 1968, but he was the reigning world champion, and he'd won Classics and the Giro d'Italia that year. He was the biggest name in cycling and the Tour de France organizers, his fans, and even the Belgian government, wanted him to ride the Tour, but Merckx said no. He wouldn't ride for the Belgian national team because his sponsor, an Italian coffee machine manufacturer called Faema, had spent a fortune building a team around him. But the Tour had to have Merckx, so the following year the rules changed, and Merckx rode the Tour de France for Faema, and he won it by miles.

BLACK, GOLD, AND RED

The 1930 Belgian Tour de France jersey was predominantly black, with a yellow and red chest band. Yellow and red cuffs were added to later versions. The jersey remained unchanged until 1940, during which time Romain Maes (1935) and Sylvère Maes (1939) won Tours for Belgium.

Romain and Sylvère Maes weren't related, but both their victories are notable. Romain wore the yellow jersey from the first to the last stage, a feat accomplished only by Ottavio Bottecchia in 1924, Nicolas Frantz in 1928, and Jacques Anquetil in 1961. And Sylvère Maes won the first mountain time

The Belgian team at stage 3 of the 1960 Tour de France, which was won by the Italian Gastone Nencini.

Action from the 2008 under-23 world road race championships in Italy, showing the current Belgian national team jersey well to the fore.

trial ever held in the Tour. It ran 40 miles (64.5 km) from Bonneville to Bourg St. Maurice, and it climbed and descended the Col d'Iseran, which at 9068 feet (2764 m) was the highest point of any Tour at the time. It was also the second of a brutal three stages in one day.

Maes also won the King of the Mountains, and the Belgians won the team classification, but it was the end of five glorious years for the Belgian team in the Tour de France. Maes was the last Belgian to win until Eddy Merckx in 1969.

OVERHEATED

According to a story on the website *The Belgian Cycling Jersey*, the Belgian rider Raymond Impanis prompted a change in the Belgian team jersey, after complaining about the design during the 1947 Tour. Impanis is on record as having said that, although he finished sixth overall in the 1947 Tour, he couldn't really challenge because the black Belgian jersey made him too hot. Impanis complained to the Belgian Cycling Federation, and the design was changed to a kingfisher-blue background with a black, yellow, and red chest band, collar, and cuffs. This design is still used by Belgian teams in the world championships today.

The Spanish National Team Jersey

1930—1990

For 60 years since its introduction in 1930, the basic design of the Spanish team jersey hardly changed. But, as with the Italian design, the Spanish federation modernized the look of its jersey. The result is that today's red and yellow national jersey, although attractive enough, lacks continuity with the original design, and some of its style.

THE JERSEYS

Vicente Trueba climbing the Col du Tourmalet during the 1933 Tour de France. The points he won at the top of the climb helped him take the first ever King of the Mountains title.

The original Spanish national team jersey had a gray background, with one yellow and one red band. Later, it changed to a gray background, with a red-yellow-red band across the chest, and the same on the collar and cuffs. The red and yellow are from the Spanish flag, where they are said to depict

the blood and sand of the bull ring. And that's how it stayed, with slight changes, through to 1990, when much bigger changes were made.

Salvador Cardena was the star of the first Spanish team in the Tour de France, but the 24-year-old Vicente Trueba, who

The 1959 Tour de France winner Federico Bahamontes, in the Spanish national team jersey, at the start of the 1960 race.

raced as an individual in Spain, generated more interest. Although very small in stature and weighing only 99 pounds (45 kg), he climbed mountains like an angel. The French press christened him the "Torrelavega Flea"—Torrelavega being the municipality where he was born. Unfortunately, Trueba wasn't a great descender, and after breaking away on many climbs he was always passed during the descent. He finished 24th overall in the 1930 Tour.

Trueba really entered the record books in 1933, when the first King of the Mountains contest was run in the Tour. Trueba won it, and finished sixth overall. Trueba was also the first Spaniard to lead the Tour over some of its most famous climbs, including the Col du Tourmalet and Col du Galibier.

THE EAGLE OF TOLEDO

The first Spaniard to win the Tour de France is also the only rider to have won it in the Spanish national team jersey. His name is Federico Bahamontes, and he proved to be one of the best mountain climbers of all time. He was so good the press named him "The Eagle of Toledo." They loved giving riders nicknames in those days, and this one was particularly inspired.

Henri Anglade at the start of the 1960 Tour de France when, after his performance the previous year, he was made leader of the French national team.

When Bahamontes attacked on a climb he was an eagle on two wheels. He soared and wheeled up the rocky slopes, leaving everyone gasping in his wake. He won the Tour de France King of the Mountains six times, and his 1959 Tour de France victory was based on his prodigious climbing powers. But it also exposed a serious flaw in the national teams format used in the world's biggest professional bike race.

One week before the 1959 Tour began, a young rider called Henri Anglade won the French national championships. Despite this, he was deemed not ready for the national team. By 1959, the Tour was also inviting regional French teams to take part, and so Anglade instead rode for a team called Centre-Midi. Anglade performed exceptionally well in the Tour's early stages, and he quickly established a huge lead over the French national team riders. By stage 18 he was second overall behind Bahamontes, and nobody from the French team was anywhere near. However, instead of attacking in an effort to close the gap, the French team conspired to help Bahamontes win. The reason? Money.

Daniel Dousset was one of the most powerful people in cycling at the time. He was a rider's agent who arranged the riders' contracts with teams, and negotiated with criterium organizers (a criterium is a race around a closed circuit), who paid for riders to do exhibition races all over Europe on small-town circuits, which the public paid to watch. Criteriums were big business, and top riders commanded large fees to ride as many as 30 or 40 of these races in the two months that followed each year's Tour de France.

The tragedy of Francisco Cepeda

Francisco Cepeda loved the Tour de France. He was the single member of the Spanish team in 1931, then raced as a touriste-routier with Vicente Trueba in the 1932 and 1933 Tours. Spain didn't send a full team owing to the political turmoil engulfing the country at the time, which would ultimately lead to the Spanish Civil War (1936–1939). Cepeda's career was cut tragically short in 1934, however, when he was killed in a mountain stage of the Tour.

The accident occurred while Cepeda was competing as part of a joint Spanish–Swiss team. He was descending quickly in wet conditions on the top part of the Col du Galibier's southern side, which joins the Lautaret pass. The route is very twisty there, and Cepeda must have gone into a bend too fast and run out of road. He crashed and cracked his head on a rock, fracturing his skull, dying three days later in hospital. He was the first rider to die during a stage of the Tour.

But Dousset had a rival, Roger Piel. He broke into the business by representing lower-profile riders, among whom was Henri Anglade. All of the French national team riders, on the other hand, belonged to Dousset. Thus Dousset, who didn't want Anglade to win, instructed the French national team to make sure that Bahamontes, who was also represented by Dousset, emerged victorious. In so doing, Dousset would get 10 percent of the Tour winner's fees. So, with the French team as well as the Spanish working for him, Bahamontes cruised to victory.

Alejandro Valverde wearing his interpretation of the Spanish national champion's jersey during the 2015 Tour de France. The "blood and sand" red and yellow national colors contrast with his Movistar team blue.

The British Tour de France Team Jersey

1955—1968

The first British team to take part in the Tour de France did so in 1955. The jerseys they wore were, like those of every other team that year, designed by the Tour de France, but, unlike the rest, they bore no resemblance to the jersey worn by British riders in other international competitions.

A NEW DESIGN

The first British Tour de France team jersey was white, with a wide black band around the chest and a thin black band around each cuff. The white collars mimicked those of a polo shirt. A rectangular Union Jack was sewn onto each sleeve.

Only two British riders finished the 1955 Tour, and it wasn't until 1960 that a wholly British team was invited again. In the intervening years, the few British riders who became part of the European pro peloton, such as Brian Robinson, competed in the

The 1990s Team GB design has echoes in today's British team jerseys.

Bradley Wiggins, whose Team Wiggins colors echo the old British national team jersey worn in all international competitions, apart from the Tour de France.

Tour as a part of mixed-nations teams. In 1958, Robinson won Britain's first stage in the Tour de France while riding for the Internations team, and the following year he won another stage with the same team.

With British cycling's stock raised by Robinson, and by other British riders who had joined him, a British team was invited to the 1960 and 1961 Tours. In those races the GB jersey was white, with two parallel black bands around the chest and black collar and cuffs. A Union Jack shield was stitched to each shoulder. The collars were round, and the jerseys had front zips, in the style of a modern cycling jersey.

In 1962, the Tour reverted to trade-sponsored teams, but the national team format returned for two years in 1967 and 1968, when the British team jersey was all-white, with two Union Jack epaulets. The jersey supplier was Le Coq Sportif, which today supplies the Tour de France leader's

jerseys. The 1967 British Tour de France team jersey will be forever associated with the death of Britain's first yellow jersey, its first winner of any of cycling's monuments, and the first British world professional road race champion—Tom Simpson.

The Great Britain jersey used in other international competitions, such as the world championships, was blue, with red sleeves. It changed to what was seen as a more modern design during the 1990s, and has evolved today into a red, white, and blue jersey that recalls the colors of the British flag.

However, many cyclists think that the original blue jersey with red sleeves was the best design, and now that retro style is very fashionable in cycling. When Sir Bradley Wiggins, a great student of cycling history, launched his own team, Team Wiggins, in 2015, he chose a design based on the older blue-with-red design jersey.

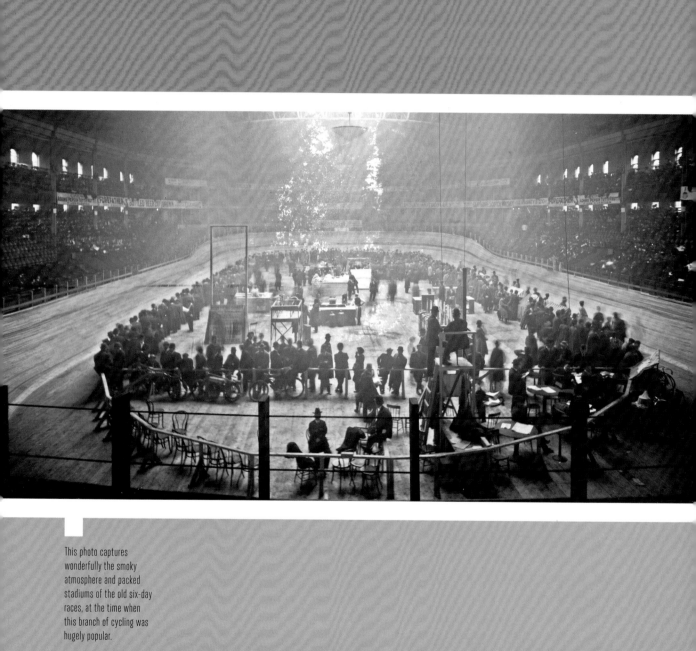

This photo captures
wonderfully the smoky
atmosphere and packed
stadiums of the old six-day
races, at the time when
this branch of cycling was
hugely popular.

TRACK JERSEYS

Without extraneous details such as pockets, and with an eye on improving aerodynamics, jerseys for track racing were designed for maximum speed. The big step forward in track jersey design occurred in the 1940s, when Armando Castelli began making silk racing jerseys for track racers. This chapter celebrates those silk jerseys, which seemed to glow, especially under the lights of a six-day race inside a noisy velodrome.

Stars and Stripes Six-Day Jersey

1948—1970s

This "Captain America"-styled jersey was first seen in Europe during the 1940s on the backs of American national track champions, such as Jack Simes II. It soon found its way into the six-day race circuit as one of the regular designs.

RIDERS FOR HIRE

Riders in six-day track races are contracted to ride on a race-to-race basis. They don't represent their normal professional teams. Instead, their jerseys are provided for each race by the race promoter. Every six-day race has its own regular jersey designs and its own sponsors. In some six-day events, the different jerseys will each carry the name of one of the sponsors. Modern six-day jerseys are made from a synthetic material that resembles silk.

Six-day jersey designers sometimes borrow from existing jerseys, as in the case of the American national champion's stars and stripes jersey. Some six-day jerseys have also been adopted by teams or races, the most famous example being the polka-dot King of the Mountains jersey in the Tour de France, which first appeared in the Paris six-day race of the 1930s, where it was seen by a young Félix Lévitan. Many years later, Lévitan became the director of the Tour de France.

The stars and stripes jersey featured here is from a 1960s Belgian six-day race because it has the black, yellow, and red Belgian national colors on its collar and cuffs. It was modeled on the American national champion's jersey, which has changed slowly over the years. Across a number of events, the American national champion today is entitled to wear a jersey that has a red and white striped lower half, a white upper, and blue sleeves with white stars on them.

The stars on this silk stars and stripes jersey aren't printed on the fabric, but are star-shaped cut-outs sewn onto it.

Action from one of the earliest six-day races held at New York's Madison Square Gardens.

TEAM NUMBERS

Six-day events are contested by teams of two. The jersey featured here was worn by a member of team six—ascertainable thanks to the team numbers stitched onto each sleeve. Within each team, the two riders' jerseys are differentiated by the color of the numbers; one features the number in a dark color, and the other in white. The same system of numbers exists today in six-day events, although the numbers are larger and often printed on the back of each jersey, as well as on the sleeves.

The numbers are integral to the enjoyment of the race spectators. Not only do they allow them to see where each team is on the track, they also allow those watching to see which rider in each team is attacking or struggling, or holding the team's position in the race.

The Madisons

The focal point of any six-day race are the Madisons, nonstop relay races that take place each day, during which the two riders in each team share the race time, one dropping out to recover, while the other takes his place. The race continues in this way for the duration, with the changeover between riders often accompanied by a mighty handsling from the rider taking over. Madisons are cycling's equivalent of tag wrestling.

Modern Six-Day Jerseys

1990–present day

Six-day races have local sponsors and, as we have seen, feature very different jersey designs, many of which have local resonance. This section of the book looks at jerseys that have featured recently in some of the oldest six-day events and looks at the history of these fascinating races.

THE MUNICH SIX-DAY JERSEYS

The first European six-day race was held in Toulouse in 1906, but it was abandoned after three days due to lack of interest. It took a while for six-day races to take hold, but, once they had, they really took hold in Germany, which is still the heartland of this cycling format.

The Munich Six-Day is one of the oldest races of its type, and it is a great example of what six-day racing is about—pure entertainment. The Munich race has a funfair outside, and restaurants and a night club inside its stadium, which is packed during what is a week-long party.

Munich jerseys include a yellow one for the race leader, and a version of the rainbow jersey for teams in which one or both members are reigning world champions. There is a nod to a rider's nation in some of the jerseys, from the obvious copy of the Italian national champion's jersey, to the less obvious white with a red chest band for Austria. Other designs are more obscure, and the team sponsors less well known, such as Stadler—the biggest two-wheeled transport center in Germany.

The black-number jersey for the team sponsored by Stadler in the Munich Six-Day.

A striking gray and orange number for team 11.

The Italian team's jersey was sponsored by the province of Emilia Romagna.

The jersey worn by a team made up of Austrian riders.

This jersey was worn by a world champion's team.

The leader's yellow jersey in the Munich Six-Day.

The Ghent Six-Day's version of the rainbow jersey, worn by the world champion's team.

exclusive experience to those who could afford it, in which bike fans enjoyed the racing while sophisticates enjoyed fine dining in track-center restaurants. But those days have passed; today's six-day races are noisy spectacles, with fast food and lots of beer.

The Ghent Six-Day, known now as the *Zesdaagse van Vlaanderen-Gent*, which means the Flanders Six-Day of Ghent, is supported by a number of the same sponsors each year, many of which are quite local. In the shirt shown here, which is worn by the world champion team, Callant is an insurance company based in eastern Flanders.

Ghent is the only six-day that Sir Bradley Wiggins has won, but if he wasn't so good at many other branches of cycling, Wiggins could have dominated six-day racing. Ghent was special to Wiggins because he was born there. His father, Gary Wiggins, who was Australian but was based in Ghent, was a six-day racer in the 1970s and '80s. Wiggins' partner at the time he won, Matthew Gilmore, also has an Australian former six-day racing father, and was also born in Ghent.

GHENT SIX-DAY JERSEYS

The first Ghent six-day race was held in 1922. Whereas all the other six-day events in Belgium have since ceased, Ghent continues to thrive. It is called the working man's six-day event as it caters for the less well-heeled. This once stood in contrast to some of the French six-day events, such as Paris and Grenoble, which offered a more

Six-day history

The first six-day race was held in 1878, in Islington's Agricultural Hall, in London. A professional cyclist, David Stanton, sought a bet that he could ride 1000 miles (1600 km) within six days, and the stake of £100 was put up by a Mr A. Davis. Stanton won the bet, covering the distance in 73 hours, but the spectacle of him riding around and around a tiny marked-out oval in a big hall proved very popular. Soon more six-day endurance tests were organized, although these were contests to see who could ride the farthest in six days. The first races were in the era of the penny-farthing. The invention of the chain-driven safety cycle led to an increase in race speeds, prompting a move to banked tracks. Indoor velodromes were built, and the sport spread to America. The first American six-day was held in Madison Square Gardens, New York, in 1891. It was a solo race and proved popular. At first America loved the macabre spectacle of exhausted riders wobbling around the track as tiredness overtook them, sometimes falling asleep on their bikes or even hallucinating because of sleep deprivation. Eventually, in an effort to make the races faster, the format was changed to two-man teams, whereby one rider raced while the other rested. Eventually the core of a six-day race became a two-man team relay, which was called the Madison, in honor of its birthplace.

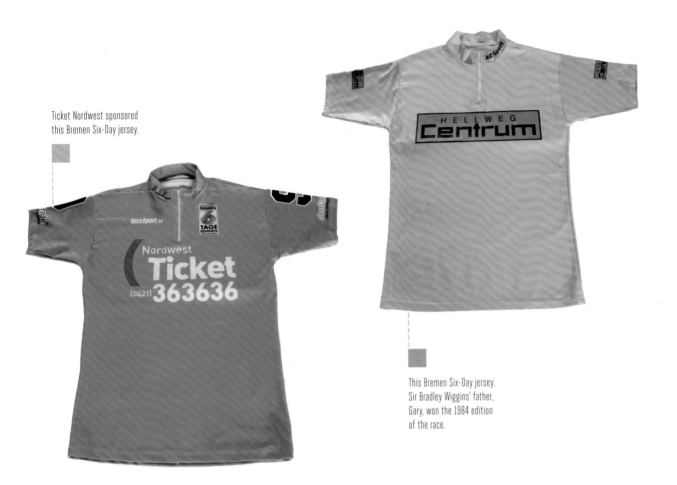

Ticket Nordwest sponsored
this Bremen Six-Day jersey.

This Bremen Six-Day jersey.
Sir Bradley Wiggins' father,
Gary, won the 1984 edition
of the race.

BREMEN SIX-DAY JERSEYS

Six-day racing was huge in Europe until
the 1980s, when it began to decline. Six-day
races are held in winter, and many top road
racers did one or two six-day events because
they were paid well to ride them. But as
road racing teams grew richer, they were
less keen on letting their stars race in
six-day events, and this led to a decline in
the six-day format, because there were
fewer big names from road racing to attract
spectators. The number of six-day races fell
as a result, but those that survived have
experienced a resurgence of interest lately.
Bremen is one of them.

One hundred and twenty-seven thousand
people paid to watch the 2015 Bremen
Six-Day, which is another with vast local
business support. Sponsors include
Bremen-based Hellweg Centrum, a massive
discount center, and Nordwest Ticket, the
Bremen version of Ticketmaster.

The jersey worn by riders in the Ghent
and Bremen six-day races are made by the
Belgian sports clothing company Nicosport,
which was started by an ex-racer, Nico
Laplage, and is run today by his son,
Lorenzo Laplage, who himself used to
be a very good six-day racer.

The Union Jack London Six-Day Jersey

1968—1979

Before the most recent London Six-Day event, held in October 2015, there had been four previous sets of races. The first two were one-offs, held in 1903 and 1923. Then there was a six-day race at the large Olympia conference center in 1934, and a run of four races at the old Empire Pool building in Wembley from 1936 to 1939, followed by a further two events in 1951 and 1952, again at Wembley. Then came the most famous set of London Six-Day races, the Skol Sixes.

THE UNION JACK DESIGN

It was during the Skol Six-Day, which ran from 1967 until 1980, that the Union Jack jersey was introduced. It quickly became the most distinctive jersey in the race, although it didn't appear until the second Skol Six, and some years it wasn't used at all. The first Skol Six was held inside the Earl's Court exhibition center in 1967. Like all the other Skol Sixes, it used a temporary track, but the track for Earl's Court was poor. For all subsequent Skol events, which were held in Wembley, a new and improved temporary track was used.

The Anglo-Australian pairing of Trevor Bull (from Birmingham, England) and Ron Baensch (from Melbourne, Australia) were the first to wear the Union Jack jersey in 1968. The last riders to do so were the

This version of the British national team jersey, which was used until 2012, echoes the design of the Union Jack London Six-Day jersey.

The London Six-Day was revived in 2015, with the British riders Ollie Woods (left) and Chris Latham taking second place overall.

British rider Maurice Burton and his New Zealand partner, Paul Medhurst, in 1979.

Only one British rider ever won the Skol Six, and that was Tony Gowland in 1972. His flashy style of racing helped make the Union Jack jersey famous, although he wasn't wearing it the year he won the race. He was partnered that year by the greatest ever six-day racer, Patrick Sercu, and it was stipulated in Sercu's 1972 Skol Six contract that he had to race in a jersey of the colors of his road team sponsor, Dreher. As they were a team, Gowland had to wear the same.

Gowland was back in the Union Jack in 1973, when he partnered Graeme Gilmore, the Australian six-day racer and father of Matthew Gilmore. Gowland and Gilmore finished fourth, the same position that Gowland finished in the following year— again in the Union Jack jersey, but this time with a German rider, Sigi Renz, as his partner.

The Brit Barry Hoban, a winner of eight stages in the Tour de France, wore the Union Jack jersey in 1974, riding with Graeme Gilmore, who is his brother-in-law. There was no Union Jack team in 1975 or 1977. In 1978, Steve Heffernan and Mick Bennett, the current race director of the Tour of Britain, wore the Union Jack design. The last Union Jack pairing, Maurice Burton and Paul Medhurst, finished sixth in the 1979 Skol Six.

Some of the 1953 Giro
d'Italia riders, left to right:
Fausto Coppi, Wim Van Est,
and Gino Bartali

1950s PRO TEAM JERSEYS

Toward the end of the 1950s, professional cycling teams changed. At the start of the decade, the only cycling sponsors permitted were bike and tire manufacturers. In the second half of the 1950s, however, the rules were relaxed to allow sponsors from outside of cycling, referred to as "extra-sportif," to have their names on jerseys. The rules still didn't allow them to be headline sponsors, although in Italy this was seemingly ignored.

Bianchi

1946–1955

Fausto Coppi is a cycling legend, one of the greats of road cycling, a man ranked with Eddy Merckx and Bernard Hinault. Like them, Coppi could win almost any race, but it was the margin and manner of Coppi's victories that made him stand out. From 1946 until 1955 he raced for the team sponsored by a Milanese car, motorbike, and bicycle manufacturer, Edoardo Bianchi. During that time, Coppi wore the color Bianchi made his own: a shade of blue called *celeste*. Almost everything Coppi touched is iconic, but nothing more than his Bianchi jersey.

The Bianchi-Campagnolo team jersey. This version of the Bianchi jersey was used by the team from 1973 to 1977.

THE RIDER

Fausto Coppi was style on wheels. Ungainly off his bike, his long legs, narrow waist and huge chest lent him the look of a man-sized stork. But on a bike, he flew. That's where the Coppi magic happened. He powered his pedals effortlessly, turning them with grace rather than force. He wasn't like other riders. There was no question of timing his attacks, of catching his rivals napping; Coppi ghosted to the front of the peloton, spun his pedals a little faster, and within seconds was gone. At the height of his power he was rarely caught. He was a superb time trialist and one of the greatest-ever climbers. He wasn't the best in a sprint, but Coppi didn't need to be. When he won he was almost always alone, and almost always minutes in front of the next rider.

His *palmarès* include two overall victories at the Tour de France (1949 and 1952) and five at the Giro d'Italia (1940, 1947, 1949, 1952, and 1953), as well as a plethora of wins in one-day classics, including the road race world championship (1953), Milan–San Remo (1946, 1948, and 1949), and Paris–Roubaix (1950). His success and his epic rivalry with Gino Bartali (see pages 111–113) brought inspiration to millions of Italians after the ravages of the Second World War.

Fausto Coppi has just taken the yellow jersey in the 1952 Tour de France. His team sponsor's name, Bianchi, is displayed on a small sewn-on patch, as was the custom then.

THE JERSEY

Edoardo Bianchi was born in 1865 under the shadow of il Duomo, the cathedral in the center of Milan. He was taken in by the Martinette orphanage, which educated him and taught him the rudiments of mechanics. Bianchi later served his apprenticeship and set up his own workshop, producing precision instruments, invalid carriages, and bicycles. His bicycle production took off,

and he was soon supplying bikes to the Italian royal family. But then came a royal command: Bianchi was asked not just to make bikes for the royals, but also to teach the princesses and other noble ladies how to ride their bikes. One of the princesses is linked to the legend of celeste—the shade of blue that was to become synonymous with Bianchi jerseys and bikes.

The ups and downs of Fausto Coppi

Coppi's career was punctuated by bone-breaking crashes, just as his life was marked by traumatic events. As a rider, there was rarely a time when he could race consistently for three years in a row. He turned pro under the shadow of the Second World War, and by the end of it was a prisoner of war. He won the Tour of Italy for a second time in 1947, then won it again and his first Tour de France in 1949. After that, Coppi fractured his pelvis in 1950, and broke his collarbone in 1951 and his scapula in 1952. He still won races, though, including the 1952 Tour de France and the 1953 world professional road race title. His personal life was scarcely any easier. His brother died after crashing in a race in 1951, and Coppi himself was shunned by the Catholic Church because his wife wouldn't divorce him and he lived with another married woman. Most tragically of all, Coppi died young. He contracted malaria in December 1959 on a visit to Burkina Faso, fell ill on his return, and was wrongly diagnosed. Coppi's life ended on January 2, 1960. He was just 40 years old.

Coppi with his brother Serse (left), just after Serse was awarded joint victory, with Frenchman André Mahé, in the 1949 Paris-Roubaix.

Well, legends really, as there are two. One holds that celeste was mixed to match the eyes of a princess Bianchi built a bike for. The other legend says that celeste is the first layer of blue above the setting sun in the Milan sky. The latter seems most likely. When the sun sets anywhere in a clear sky, where the red and orange shades become blue, that blue is celeste.

Bianchi team bikes have always been celeste, and whenever the company has been the lead sponsor of a team, their jersey, like Coppi's, has been celeste and white.

Period features

The original Bianchi jersey had a shirt collar, making it look rather like a polo shirt. This was pure fashion and served no practical purpose. The first cycling jerseys didn't have collars; they were added in the late 1930s. This fashion persisted until the early 1960s, at which point shirt collars were replaced with round-cuff collars, very similar to those of today.

Celeste is to cycling what Ferrari red is to motor sport. A long line of champions has raced in Bianchi celeste, but the most famous is Fausto Coppi, raising his jersey to a work of art.

In 1949, the Bianchi team was co-sponsored by Ursus, a Polish tractor manufacturer trying to open new markets after the Second World War. All jerseys used by professional riders during this time were made from fine merino wool, and sponsors' names were embroidered onto them. The block of color with a contrasting chest band is a classic cycling jersey design that has staged a fashion comeback in recent times, so this jersey still looks modern.

What aren't modern, however, are the two chest pockets. Most road racing jerseys had them right up until the 1960s. Modern cycling jerseys still have back pockets, located just above the hip, for riders to carry food and other essentials. Front jersey pockets reflect the generally longer race distances of Coppi's era, and the fact that riders took extra food with them because they weren't allowed to drop back to their team support cars and take more, like they do now.

One of Fausto Coppi's legendary Bianchi race bikes.

Bartali-Ursus

1951

Bartali-Ursus was one of the teams sponsored by the great Gino Bartali's bike company. From 1949 until his retirement in 1954, Bartali raced for the team to promote his brand. He was the prewar Italian cycling superstar, before the emergence of Fausto Coppi, and their rivalry was one of the major talking points of Italian cycling.

THE JERSEY

Ursus was one of many cosponsors Bartali linked up with to fund his team. Although there is an engineering company in Italy today called Ursus—they make, among other things, lightweight wheels for racing bikes—this was founded in 1967. The Ursus on the Bartali-Ursus jersey is in fact a Polish tractor manufacturer, which, during the 1950s, was looking to break into the Italian market.

The Bartali-Ursus jersey was all yellow, with a blue collar and a blue band near the bottom of the sleeves. After a bad cycling crash, Bartali stopped racing in 1954 at the age of 40. Afterward, he took over the management of his team, and continued for many years in that role, even after he stopped sponsoring it. Toward the end

of 1959, when Bartali was running a team for San Pellegrino, he signed up his great rival, Fausto Coppi, who by then was 40 years old but looking for one more year as a rider. That never happened, because Coppi contracted malaria toward the end of the year and died early in 1960.

Gino Bartali in 1952, when he raced for his own team, sponsored by his own bike brand, and was Italian national road race champion.

Bartali leading his greatest rival, Fausto Coppi, during the 1949 Tour de France. It's stage 17 and they are climbing the Petit St. Bernard Pass.

THE RIVALRY

When Fausto Coppi turned pro in 1940, Gino Bartali, who was five years older, was an established star, having recorded Tour de France and Giro d'Italia victories. Coppi signed for Bartali's then team, Legnano, and so began a famous rivalry.

At first, everything between the two riders was good; Coppi won the 1940 Giro d'Italia with Bartali's blessing and support. However, this changed during an important Italian race, the Giro dell'Emilia, after Bartali accused Coppi of double-crossing him. Coppi had said he felt unwell, but promised he would nevertheless still attack early to tire Bartali's rivals, sacrificing his chances while Bartali conserved his energy. But when Coppi sustained the attack and

went on to win, the claim of ill health rang hollow, and Bartali felt tricked. "I thought you were ill," Bartali shouted at Coppi after the race. "I was but the race made me feel better," Coppi replied lamely.

As far as Bartali was concerned, their bond of trust was broken, and after the Second World War they became rivals in different teams. Bartali admired Coppi's talent, although he studied him for weaknesses, and eventually found one he could exploit. Bartali reckoned that when Coppi wasn't having a good day a vein would swell on his right leg. So he had a teammate follow Coppi in races to watch his legs, and when the team mate shouted, "Gino, the vein," Bartali attacked, and won.

It soon became clear to everyone, however, that Coppi was better than Bartali, and this fact made Bartali suspicious. He thought Coppi must be enhancing his performance somehow, with a magic potion or even a drug. Bartali slowly became paranoid, and had bottles Coppi had drunk from analyzed to see what was in them. He even started sneaking into Coppi's hotel rooms and searching for incriminating evidence. Eventually the mistrust spread to the fans of Coppi and Bartali, and both riders were suspended by the Italian Cycling Federation for quitting the 1948 world road race championships, rather than support each other. Yet their rivalry rumbled on until the following year's Tour de France.

Bartali (left) with the first ever Dutch yellow jersey, Wim Van Est, in 1951.

Righteous Among Nations

A deeply religious man, Bartali was known as Gino the Pious. During the Second World War, Bartali used his training rides to deliver documents for the Italian Resistance. He also helped Jews escape from the country, first by transporting forged documents to them, and on one occasion hiding a Jewish family in his cellar. The authorities suspected what he was doing but were scared to stop him, because they feared provoking unrest in Tuscany, where he was adored. Eventually, he was arrested and interrogated by the Italian SS. He admitted nothing, and the experience made him more determined to help victims of the war, in particular Italian Jews.

After the war Bartali never spoke of any of this, not even to his family. It was only discovered in 2010, when a Jewish accountant from Pisa, Giorgio Nissim, died and his sons read their father's diaries. In them were all the details of Bartali's heroics. In 2013 the Jewish organization Yad Vashem awarded Bartali the title of Righteous Among Nations, given to foreigners who risked their lives for Jews during the Holocaust.

At home in 1963, Bartali smoked even during his racing career, saying that a cigarette or two in the evening calmed his nerves during stage races.

DECISIVE BREAKAWAY

Bartali was unstinting in his support of Coppi in the 1949 Tour, but early in the race Coppi seemed out of sorts, which angered Bartali. Then on stage 16, a big ride through the Alps, something clicked and he and Bartali dominated the day. And, with a good lead established, Coppi let Bartali win the stage and take the yellow jersey on his birthday. The next day, in Aosta, Italy, Coppi went on his own, winning by five minutes from Bartali. The race was won; Coppi went even farther ahead, and eventually won the Tour by ten minutes from Bartali. He was the best. Bartali knew it, and the rivalry was over, though he still won a stage in the 1950 Tour de France, and the 1952 Italian national road race championships. His last big win was a stage of the 1954 Giro d'Italia.

Nivea-Fuchs

1954—1956

Nivea-Fuchs was a landmark team thanks in large part to Nivea, the first company from outside cycling to become the headline sponsor of a professional team. Nivea also stands out because of the lovely irony that the star of the team, just about the toughest rider in cycling, was publicizing a moisturizer.

THE THIRD MAN

The star was Fiorenzo Magni, known as *Il Leone di Fiandre*, the Lion of Flanders, for the very un-Italian but unique feat of winning the Tour of Flanders three years in a row. Magni won in 1949, 1950, and 1951, and nobody has ever repeated his achievement in this great cobbled classic.

In many respects, Magni was the "third man" of the golden era of Italian cycling. He was unfortunate perhaps to have had his career at the same time as Gino Bartali and Fausto Coppi. Magni was indeed a man of threes, because, as well as three Tours of Flanders, he won the Giro d'Italia three times (in 1948, 1951, and 1955) and was Italian national champion three times (1951, 1953, and 1954).

Nivea was associated with Magni as a personal sponsor long before it sponsored a team, but moving to principal sponsorship helped save Italian pro cycling. Before the Second World War, far more bikes were manufactured than cars, and there were far more bikes on Italian roads even in the early 1950s. Then the rebirth of the Italian engineering industry took hold, and the country entered a more modern age. People wanted cars and scooters, not bikes.

A 16-year-old Fiorenzo Magni, taken at the very start of his cycling career in 1936, when he was still a junior racer.

Magni (center) in the 1950 Tour de France. He was leading when Gino Bartali withdrew the Italian team because French fans had threatened and assaulted him.

The Italian cycle industry began to suffer as sales dwindled, and sponsoring a cycling team became a big drain on the bottom line. People still loved watching big races, but they weren't buying bikes, so company accountants started questioning the financial sense of team sponsorship. This prompted Fiorenzo Magni to ask his personal sponsor to take over a team. Nivea agreed, and made a deal with the Swiss bike manufacturer Fuchs. The age of extra-sportif sponsorship began.

Taking after the jersey worn by the Italian national team in the world championships, the Nivea-Fuchs jersey was all blue, with white writing. Fiorenzo Magni wore that jersey for the 1956 Giro d'Italia, during which photographs were taken of him that have become some of the most iconic in the history of cycling. That Tour was to be his last.

Magni crashed on stage 12 of the Giro d'Italia and broke his right collarbone. Although he was able to withstand the pain enough to continue racing, he was unable to pull on his handlebars with his right arm. Instead, Magni improvised magnificently. His mechanic cut an inner tube out of an old tire and tied one end to Magni's handlebars. When Magni needed extra leverage, he put the other end between his teeth, and pulled on that.

GS Carpano

1956–1965

GS Carpano was created in 1956 to support Fausto Coppi in the final period of his career. It also helped Coppi sell his own brand of bikes, which the team rode for its first two years. Carpano later took over as sole sponsor, and so became the first business from outside cycling to sponsor a team on its own. Others followed during the 1960s, with greater or lesser support from cycle and tire manufacturers.

Carpano is the original vermouth, and the creation of Antonio Benedetto Carpano (1764–1815). Carpano invented vermouth in Turin in 1786, making it from white wine, over 30 different herbs, and a dash of spirits for sweetness. It was a popular drink, and the company continued long after Carpano's death. Eventually, like so many firms in the drinks industry, Carpano was taken over in 2001 by the much larger Distillerie Fratelli Branca in Milan.

The name was preserved, though, and Carpano vermouth, and variations of it, are still produced today.

The GS Carpano jersey design is based on the uniform of Turin's Juventus soccer team, thanks to Carpano's team manager, Vincenzo Giacotto, who was a huge Juventus fan. The first Carpano jerseys had polo-shirt collars, but as the team went into the next decade, it copied the round collars with short zippers of other teams' jerseys.

Carpano was an excellent team, with the best equipment and well-paid riders. Coppi was the big name for the first few years, but he didn't win much. Another aging star, Ferdi Kübler, won Milan–Turin in 1956, which was a big deal for a Turin-based company. The other victories came from a small contingent of Belgians.

Nino Defilippis was a favorite Carpano rider because he came from Turin, where the team was based.

Italo Zilioli rode for Carpano for the first three years of his career, 1962 to 1964, and is another rider from Turin who enjoyed riding in the same colors as Juventus.

After the success of 1956, the team increased its Belgian contingent for the following year, adding manpower and also quality, in the shape of Fred De Bruyne. De Bruyne won the Tour of Flanders and Paris–Roubaix in 1957. The following year he won Liège–Bastogne–Liège, and repeated the feat again in 1959. He stopped racing at the end of the 1960 season and his position as top Carpano rider was taken by Nino Defilippis in 1961. He was the vivacious, very stylish son of a rich Turin businessman, and a fast sprinter who became a good classics racer. Defilippis was Italian national champion in 1960 and 1962, and he won a number of stages in the Giro d'Italia for Carpano.

Carpano was one of a number of apéritif producers to be involved in cycling. Others included Cynar from Italy and the French company Saint-Raphaël, who had a great team in the 1960s. In fact, it is not uncommon to have sponsorship from several companies in the same sector at the same time, at least in team sponsorship. At different times, there have been multiple sponsors from kitchen equipment, ice-cream, banks, and insurance companies. And even today, when pro cycling is a global sport, there are three European lottery companies among the 20 teams that make up the world tour.

Cilo

1950—1980s

Cilo was a Swiss bike manufacturer that was involved in team sponsorship for over 30 years. Some of the best Swiss cyclists rode its beautiful handbuilt bikes. The early Cilo teams were also a great example of how pro cycling used to work, with some riders contracted on a race-to-race basis, so during one season they might ride for three or four different teams.

FREELANCING

Today the rules governing contracts between riders and teams stipulate that the shortest a contract can be is 12 months, and in that time the rider can only race for the team he or she has signed for, and only wear its approved race clothing. It was very different in the 1950s, when it was common for riders to race on a freelance basis for several different teams in the same year.

That's how the British pioneer pro Brian Robinson came to ride for the Cilo-St. Raphaël team in 1956. Robinson was one of the two riders who finished the 1955 Tour de France as part of the first British team to compete in the race. He started in 1955 as part of Hercules, the first British pro team to be based in Europe, but when that disbanded, Robinson stayed on the continent, riding freelance.

Brian Robinson (left) and teammate Fred Krebs, riding for the British team in the 1955 Tour de France. Robinson rode for the Cilo-St. Raphaël team the following year.

Hugo Koblet (center) in the pink jersey of the 1953 Giro d'Italia. He eventually finished second to the man on the right, Fausto Coppi.

"You needed contacts to get in," he explained during an interview with *Cycling Weekly* in 2014. "I joined forces with a French guy, Raymond Louviot, who'd just stopped racing and wanted to become a team manager. He got a few of us together and hired us out for races. Through Louviot I got a contract to ride the Tour of Spain, which started in April in those days, for Cilo, whose star rider was the Swiss Tour de France winner Hugo Koblet. The idea was, I would support Koblet in the race, but he wasn't going well and I ended up eighth overall, higher than Koblet finished. Because I rode so well, and because at that time Cilo was cosponsored by St. Raphaël, I ended up with a full contract with the main St. Raphaël team after the 1956 Tour de France finished. That took me to the end of the year, but St. Raphaël signed me up for the whole of 1957, and that was me in. I stayed with the St. Raphaël team for the rest of my pro career."

THE JERSEY

The Cilo jersey is a classic design that never changed while Cilo was the headline sponsor. It looked just as good in the 1980s, when Beat Breu was winning stages in the Tour de France, as it had on the shoulders of Hugo Koblet in the 1950s. The only thing that changed was the material it was made from. The 1950s Cilo jerseys were made from merino wool, nicely styled and manufactured by Vittore Gianni in Italy. But by the 1980s Switzerland was at the forefront of race clothing manufacture with Assos, who invented the skinsuit and other aerodynamic cycling gear.

Descente was another brand with a Swiss influence. It was founded in Japan, and made clothing for many sports. In 1970 the company hired Swiss aerodynamicists Hannes Keller and Hans Hess to help refine its downhill and speed-skating suits. Later, Descente switched to producing aerodynamic cycling gear. The 1980s Cilo team was supplied by Descente.

Beat Breu winning the 1982 Tour de France stage to Alpe d'Huez on his lightweight climbing bike, which was made from ultra-thin steel, with plastic replacing some metal parts.

Swiss role

Beat Breu is unique. In 1982 he won two Tour de France mountain stages wearing the Cilo-Aufina jersey. On the face of it, Breu was the archetypal climber—skinny, almost translucently pale, and obsessive about his sport—but he climbed like very few climbers do. He didn't dance uphill; instead, he hauled himself up using big gears, which made you think his legs would break. He was also a very good cyclo-cross rider, and he took third place in the 1988 world championships. He was fourth in the cyclo-cross world championship the following year, but he was also fourth in the 1988 world motor-paced championships on the track. He later became a top mountain biker, gave duathlon a go, and even became a circus clown after he stopped racing.

LE PÉDALEUR DE CHARME

Le pédaleur de charme (The Charming Pedaler) was the name given by French music hall artist Jacques Grello to the splendidly dapper Hugo Koblet, the Swiss winner of the 1951 Tour de France. The name suited him perfectly. Koblet pedaled without apparent effort, never grimacing, and he even sweated with style—he never had a hair out of place and kept a comb and a sponge soaked in cologne in his jersey pocket with which to spruce up mid-race.

In 1950, Koblet became the first non-Italian to win the Giro d'Italia, then he dominated the 1951 Tour de France. Shortly after winning the Tour, Koblet was invited to Mexico to make public appearances during a big stage race, but he came back ill, and he was never the same again.

Despite failing strength, Koblet continued to earn good money through the 1950s. He was popular, and he had personal sponsorship from Pirelli and Alfa Romeo, but behind the scenes he suffered depression brought on by a chaotic financial situation. He stopped racing in 1961, his marriage broke up, and the tax authorities began making demands.

His life was in a mess when, in 1964, Koblet was killed in a car crash. According to the only eye witness, it could have been suicide. She saw Koblet drive his white Alfa Romeo past a big tree on the Zürich–Esslingen road, stop, turn around, drive past the tree again in the other direction, stop, turn around again, and drive directly into the tree. He died from his injuries four days later.

Hugo Koblet in 1956, when his life was beginning to unravel and he wasn't the racer he had been.

Tebag

1948–1957

Tebag was a Swiss bike manufacturer whose top race bikes were painted a deep red color, giving rise to team jerseys of the same color. Tebag had the best Swiss riders in its team at one time or another, but the man most identified with the jersey is the winner of the 1950 Tour de France, Ferdi Kübler.

Ferdi Kübler (left) in the Tebag team uniform on his way to winning La Flèche Wallonne in 1951. The other rider is Gino Bartali, who finished second.

FERDI THE COWBOY

At the age of 96, Kübler is the oldest living Tour de France winner. Whereas the other great Swiss rider of the 1950s, Hugo Koblet, was introverted and had an impeccable riding style, Kübler was an extrovert who rode like he was in a fight with his bike. He was talented, though, and extremely strong. He would often attack when least expected, which sometimes brought him spectacular success, but more often didn't.

Ferdi Kübler, with his Swiss teammates, carrying the Tebag sponsorship on his Swiss national team jersey during the 1954 Tour de France.

He turned professional in 1940 and immediately started winning races. He rode for the Cilo team at first, and then for Egli Rad, but as soon as Tebag had a team, Kübler joined it. Later on, the company produced a top-of-the-range Ferdi Kübler Spezial race bike, which sold in the thousands. Unlike many other top riders of Kübler's era, who happily signed the single-team contracts offered to the best performers, Kübler freely chose a more freelance approach. He often rode major Italian races for an Italian team, but Tebag was his default choice the rest of the time.

Kübler won the Swiss road race title four times, he was world road race champion in 1956, and he won both Ardennes Classics—Flèche Wallonne and Liège–Bastogne–Liège—two years in a row, in 1951 and 1952. In 1954 he was second overall in the Tour de France, and he won the green jersey. He was known as "The Cowboy" during his career, which was the name pros usually reserved for inept riders, but in Küber's case it was because he loved wearing Stetson hats. He was a larger than life figure off and on the bike, given to making predictions, often true, that he would win, and even telling his competitors where he intended to attack. Sometimes, though, his exuberance, and predictions, got the better of him.

THE JERSEY

The Tebag jersey was a design classic. It was deep red, with white chest and arm bands, and a white polo-shirt collar. Tebag was the only name on the jersey for many years, and it was embroidered on the white chest band and both arm bands in black cotton. In later years, the collar was deep red too.

EMI-Guerra

1959—1960

As an electrical manufacturer and music publisher, EMI's involvement in cycling is a great example of the changes taking place in team sponsorship during the second half of the 1950s. The old model, whereby headline sponsorship was reserved for bike manufacturers, was becoming obsolete, even though the rules regarding sponsorship from outside cycling were strict. How the rules were enforced depended on which country the team was based in. Italy was quite relaxed, while other countries were less so. In the next chapter we'll see some of the imaginative ways teams got around the rules, particularly in France.

ANGEL OF THE MOUNTAINS

EMI-Guerra was created for Charly Gaul, a tiny Luxembourg rider nicknamed the "Angel of the Mountains." Gaul was a superb climber, who really looked like he had wings on his feet. He used lower gears than his rivals, and once the road tipped upwards, Gaul pedaled at such an infernal rhythm it was wise to let him go. Only the foolhardy tried to hang on, and they paid with even greater time losses, particularly when Gaul was at the peak of his powers. When conditions favored him—he performed best in poor weather conditions—Gaul was unbeatable. He won the 1956 Giro d'Italia with one incredible attack in appalling weather. With three days to go Gaul was lying 24th overall, 16 minutes behind the race leader, but the next stage was 150 miles (242 km) long, with several high mountain passes. It was freezing cold, with rain turning to snow whenever the riders climbed, but Gaul was oblivious to it all. As other riders became adversely affected by the conditions, Gaul waited until the final climb, Monte Bondone.

Charly Gaul in 1959. The Angel of the Mountains even looked angelic, but he could have a foul temper.

Gaul doing what he was best at, climbing mountains in adverse conditions. This shot is from the 1959 Giro d'Italia, which Gaul won.

When he got to its slopes, Gaul upped the pace and was quickly alone. At 7½ miles (12 km), Bondone is not a long climb, but Gaul managed not only to eliminate the lead of his rivals but take a big enough lead himself to win the Giro overall, despite stopping halfway up to drink hot coffee and change his freezing clothes. The effort cost him, though; Gaul couldn't walk by the end of the stage, which took him nine hours to complete. Only 49 of the morning's 89 starters made it to the finish. It was a day that made grown men cry.

Gaul did the same in the 1958 Tour de France, gaining time and then losing it, until a stage in the Chartreuse, when, again in terrible cold, wet conditions, he put on another virtuoso performance, winning enough time in one stage to win the Tour de France.

THE JERSEY

The EMI jersey, worn here by Charly Gaul, was a trendsetter. Its modern design is contrasted here with the more traditional design of Jacques Anquetil's Helyett-Leroux jersey.

Gaul had his best years with the Faema-Guerra team, under the management of Learco Guerra. It was Guerra who approached EMI to take over headline sponsorship of his team, and as was proper with a company involved in a modern business like electronics, the team jersey had a very modern design. It certainly bucked the trend of other 1950s team jerseys.

The company logo—the letters "EMI" outlined by a black diamond—took pride of place on the chest and sleeves, while the body of the jersey was white with blue hoops. The sleeves were white with blue cuffs. EMI-Guerra only existed for two years, but the blue hooped design was resurrected in the 1980s by the Atala team.

ENEMIES

By 1959, Charly Gaul had made quite a few enemies. He was a delight to watch when he raced, but less delightful to know. He was often rude to fellow racers and developed a reputation for meanness. He rarely shared what he won with teammates, which bucked a tradition in the peloton. In the 1957 Giro d'Italia, Gaul stopped for what the newspapers used to call "a natural break," and when he did, two of his rivals, Louison Bobet and Gastone Nencini, attacked. That was a breach of pro racer's etiquette, but the French papers made light of it, calling Gaul "Monsieur Pi-Pi." Later on, Gaul threatened Bobet, reminding him that he used to be a butcher and he still knew how to use a knife.

Revenge, and especially revenge on the French, partly fueled Gaul's attacks during his successful 1958 Tour de France and 1959 Giro d'Italia. As he got older and his climbing power diminished, however, he became increasingly paranoid. Gaul finished third in the 1960 Giro d'Italia and fourth in 1961, when he also finished third in the Tour de France. It was his last good result. Increasingly, Gaul thought that the other top riders were conspiring against him, which actually wasn't far from the truth.

The 1959 Giro d'Italia

The 1959 Giro d'Italia was Charly Gaul's best win for EMI-Guerra, and it was another competition in which Gaul left it late to win. The new star of France, the 1957 Tour de France winner Jacques Anquetil, led the 1959 Giro by four minutes at the start of the penultimate stage, which went from Aosta to Courmayeur. The stage crossed into France to climb the Col du Petit St. Bernard, which is exactly the sort of mountain climb that suited Charly Gaul.

The average gradient of the Petit St. Bernard is only 5 percent, but it is almost 19 miles (30 km) long and ascends 4500 feet (1400 m), finishing at 7200 feet (2200 m). Despite its physical demands, the climb suited Gaul; he could click into his rhythm and go for it. He hit the bottom of the climb hard, spinning his low gear at close to 19 mph (30 kph), and he held it there for the entire length of the climb. One by one, his opposition melted away. Anquetil, who could suffer like no other, was the last to stay with Gaul. But 2 miles (3 km) from the summit, he cracked, and did so to such an extent that, by the time he finished, he had lost seven minutes on Gaul. He was almost ten minutes down on Gaul by the finish in Courmayeur. The Angel of the Mountains had won another Grand Tour with one incredible day.

Gastone Nencini, seen here after winning the 1960 Tour de France, was one of a number of riders Charly Gaul made enemies of after one of his unpleasant outbursts.

The riders and staff of the 1967 Tour de France observe one minute's silence on July 14, the day after Tom Simpson's death. Left to right, Felice Gimondi, Jacques Goddet, Félix Lévitan, Roger Pingeon, Barry Hoban, and Vin Denson.

THE SWINGING SIXTIES

For some, the 1960s was the golden age of pro cycling, one that featured some iconic jerseys. They drew on fifties style, but with more vivid color—a feature we are able to appreciate now because of the advancement of color photography during this decade. And of course, the 1960s had its own legends—men who added another layer to the story of the cycling jersey.

Peugeot-BP-Michelin

1963—1986

The Peugeot-BP-Michelin jersey is a design classic. In the age of bold colors, Peugeot went for black and white, and was rewarded with a jersey that stood out against the others. It is still recognizable today, 30 years after it was last worn in the peloton. Peugeot also had the longest continuous involvement of any sponsor in top-level pro cycling.

START THE CHAIN

Peugeot—of Peugeot bikes, rather than the car manufacturer—had the longest involvement in top-level cycling team sponsorship. After Peugeot withdrew its sponsorship, the team continued with other sponsors until 2008. Peugeot sponsored individuals and small teams from the start of professional cycling, and some early Tour de France winners rode Peugeot bikes. However, it was in 1935 that Peugeot's sponsorship started in earnest with the formation of the Peugeot-Hutchinson team. The following year, Peugeot linked up with Dunlop and created a team that lasted until 1955. Notable victories included Ferdi Kübler's Swiss road race title and Bernardo Ruiz's victory in the Vuelta a España, both in 1948. Camille Danguillaume won the 1949 Liège–Bastogne–Liège, and Charles Coste the Grand Prix des Nations in the same year.

In 1956, Peugeot cosponsored a small Spanish team with Minaco, before establishing the Peugeot-BP-Dunlop team, which ran from 1957 to 1962. Rik Van Steenbergen won the 1957 world road race title, and Pino Cerami won Paris–Roubaix in 1960.

Perhaps the most recognizable cycling jersey ever, the black and white Peugeot-BP-Michelin team jersey of 1963–1975.

Tom Simpson in a Peugeot all-blue tracksuit just before the start of the first stage of the 1966 Tour de France.

THE JERSEY

Up until 1962, the Peugeot team jersey was a series of slightly differing variations of blue, with a yellow chest band and yellow sleeves. In 1963, the company decided to strengthen its team and change its colors. Thus, the iconic jersey design was born. It was white, with black collar and cuffs, and three rows of black and white squares in the lower half. With BP as cosponsor, the jerseys had a BP logo stitched onto each sleeve. The logos were made from a stiff black felt shaped as a shield, with BP embroidered on each in gold-colored cotton.

This was the jersey worn by Tom Simpson when he won Milan–San Remo, Bordeaux–Paris, and many other races. Simpson also won the 1965 world championships and Il Lombardia while he was with Peugeot-BP, but for those he wore the British national and the rainbow jerseys. Likewise, Roger Pingeon was contracted to Peugeot-BP when he won the 1967 Tour de France, but he was riding for the French national team when he did so.

Peugeot-BP was also the team that Eddy Merckx had his first big professional victories with. He won Milan–San Remo in 1966 and 1967, and the 1967 Flèche Wallonne for Peugeot-BP, while Tom Simpson and Merckx scored a memorable one-two for the team in the 1967 Paris–Nice.

EVOLVING PARTNERSHIPS

Peugeot-BP-Michelin was the team name until the end of 1975, a year in which Bernard Thévenet scored the biggest victory so far for the black and white Peugeots, when he won the Tour de France, bringing to an end Eddy Merckx's domination of the sport. The following year, Esso replaced Peugeot as an extra-sportif sponsor, but the only difference in jersey design was swapping the BP logo for that of Esso.

Bernard Thévenet won the 1977 Tour de France for the team. Shell replaced Esso on the sleeves in 1982, but a bigger change occurred in 1988, when Peugeot stepped aside, and the French children's clothing retailer Z took over. And so the Z-Peugeot team was formed, but it had virtually the same riders, managers, and support staff as the previous year's team had had.

Bernard Thévenet won the Tour de France for Peugeot in 1975 and 1977. The cuffs on his jersey bear red, white, and blue bands, indicating that Thévenet is a former French champion.

The foreign legion

That was the name an Australian journalist, Rupert Guinness, used for the band of British, Australian, and Irish riders who graduated from Peugeot's amateur team, ACBB, to the Peugeot pro team. The first was Graham Jones of Manchester in 1979. He was followed in 1980 by the Scottish racer Robert Millar and Phil Anderson from Australia. Irishman Stephen Roche joined Peugeot-Esso-Michelin in 1981, and won Paris–Nice in his first year. In 1982 the team swapped the Esso logo for Shell. Another Brit, Sean Yates, joined in 1982, followed by another Aussie, Allan Peiper, in 1983. That was the year Phil Anderson won Australia's first classic, the Amstel Gold Race. Robert Millar won mountain stages in the 1983 and 1984 Tour de France for the team. He also finished fourth overall in the 1984 Tour, and won the King of the Mountains.

Adrian Timmis and Joey McLoughlin rode for Z-Peugeot in 1988, and Robert Millar joined Z in 1989, after riding for the Panasonic team. From 1994 onward, Chris Boardman was the star of the Gan teams, and he continued into the first two years of Crédit Agricole. Sir Bradley Wiggins spent 2004 and 2005 racing for that team.

Graham Jones was the first of the "Foreign Legion" of British, Irish, and Australian riders to join the Peugeot team.

It was the same in 1989, when Peugeot dropped out of sponsorship for a while. Z signed Greg LeMond for 1990, and he won the Tour de France. In 1992 the team was called Z-LeMond, and in 1993 Z was replaced by the insurance company Gan, which had sponsored a big team in the 1970s. In 1998, Gan was replaced by a French bank, Crédit Agricole, but the team continued with the same manager, Roger

Legeay, who had overseen the transition from Z-Peugeot to Crédit Agricole. Legeay, who was a Peugeot rider throughout his racing career, had taken over a management and support staff structure that had links all the way back to the 1935 Peugeot-Hutchinson team. The era came to an end only when Legeay couldn't find a sponsor to take over after Crédit Agricole pulled out in 2008.

Mercier-BP-Hutchinson

1954—1969

Mercier, a French bike manufacturer, sponsored teams of varying forms from 1935 until 1983. In terms of its history and longevity, it rivals Peugeot. The Mercier and Peugeot teams were "old-school" in terms of pro cycling; they had a rigid management structure and followed the old sponsorship rules, which stated that the headline sponsor must be a cycle manufacturer, but that the team could also have a tire manufacturer as a sponsor. One extra-sportif sponsor was allowed, which, for Mercier and Peugeot in the 1950s and '60s, was BP.

A 1964 Mercier-BP-Hutchinson jersey worn by Robert Poulot. He was a pro cyclist for only two years, then worked for French customs as a border patrol officer in the Pyrenees.

M ercier's first team was called Mercier-Hutchinson. Its colors were all-purple with white lettering, and fans called the team "Les Violets." In 1950, gold-colored collars and cuffs were added. In 1954, gold sleeves and purple cuffs were introduced to help the BP shield logo stand out. Mercier-BP was one of the first teams to adopt a more modern round neck, as opposed to polo-shirt collars.

SPONSORSHIP RULES

From 1954, the team name changed to Mercier-BP-Hutchinson, reflecting a sponsorship deal that complied exactly with the cycling authorities' rules. Main sponsorship from Mercier was supplemented by support from Hutchinson, a tire manufacturer, and BP, the extra-sportif sponsor.

There were also rules about the size of lettering on cycling clothing. From 1954, the headline sponsor's name could have a maximum height of $3\frac{1}{8}$ inches (8 cm), while the cosponsor's name was limited to a height of $1^3/_{16}$ inches (3 cm) and had to be below the headline sponsor. Only two lines

André Darrigade (left) outsprints Mercier-BP's Frans Melckenbeeck to win stage two of the 1962 Tour de France, which finished in Herentals, Belgium.

of lettering were allowed, and they were permitted on the front and rear of each jersey. The size of the extra-sportif sponsor's name or logo was also controlled, and it was permitted only on the sleeves or, in certain cases, on the chest. No other lettering was allowed on the jersey—nothing on the sides or shoulders—and writing on the shorts had to go around the legs, not up them.

The rules were gradually relaxed over the years, though change was slow. It wasn't until the late 1980s that jerseys began to look the way they do today, with lettering on side panels, shoulders, and elsewhere. And change was achieved mostly by teams pushing the boundaries of what was permitted, rather than by initiatives from the authorities.

The Mercier-BP-Hutchinson team operated between 1954 and 1969, during which time changes were made to the sponsorship rules. These were prompted by the desire of teams to maximize revenue by prioritizing the more lucrative extra-sportif sponsorship over that of bike manufacturers. Of all the national cycling federations, the French authorities were the most resistant to change, but after mild provocation from the St. Raphaël team (see pages 138–141), they eventually allowed extra-sportif companies to take over as headline sponsors. The drinks companies St. Raphaël, Pelforth, and Margnat were the first, and in 1969 a Spanish white goods manufacturer, Fagor, became headline sponsor of the Mercier team, creating Fagor-Mercier-Hutchison. The team colors remained purple and gold.

Britain's Barry Hoban, third in line, was a long-time Mercier rider, recording all of his eight Tour de France stage victories with Mercier-sponsored teams.

A TALE OF TWO ZIPPERS

Mercier-BP's team manager was a legend. His name was Antonin Magne, and he had been a great bike racer in his day, the winner of the 1931 and 1934 Tour de France and the world road race title in 1936. However, he was rather withdrawn, uncommunicative, and notoriously mean. It was said that he could peel an orange in his pocket, rather than let anybody see him and have them ask him for a segment.

Antonin Magne as a racer in 1931, the year he won his first of two Tours de France.

He took that stinginess into team management. Although Magne was spending his sponsors' money, rather than his own, he didn't spend anything unnecessarily. He was fair with wages, paying most of his riders good salaries, but the equipment they were given was not the highest quality, and they didn't get a lot of it.

The British rider Barry Hoban turned professional for Mercier-BP in 1964, and he remembers what Magne was like. "I got 21 pounds per week in my first year, and with a share of the team's prize money that made 60 to 70 pounds a week, when a Manchester United soccer player would get 20 pounds, so it wasn't bad. But for clothing we got one tracksuit, two long-sleeved jerseys, four short-sleeve jerseys, six pairs of shorts, and that was it.

"We were given other jerseys as and when we required them, but we had to pay for any extra shorts we needed. But the thing about Mercier's jerseys, the quality was okay but they didn't have a zip [zipper] neck. You could get two types of racing jersey in those days, ones with a zip and ones without. The ones without a zip were one French franc cheaper, so Magne bought them. It took us years of sweltering in the Tour de France in zipless wool jerseys before Magne relented and bought jerseys with zips."

Man of Mercier

Raymond Poulidor is the name most cycling fans will associate with Mercier-BP. He spent his entire career with Mercier teams, starting in 1961 with Mercier-BP-Hutchinson, and ending with Miko-Mercier in 1977. When he raced, Poulidor was the most popular cyclist in France; he maybe still is, but it wasn't because he won. He was the ultimate underdog, beaten by Jacques Anquetil during the 1960s and again by Eddy Merckx in the '70s. Poulidor tried, and failed, repeatedly to win, but he kept smiling, and the public loved him for it.

Poulidor was also Antonin Magne's blindspot. The Mercier manager might have been ungenerous with the rest of the team, but Poulidor could have anything. Magne had discovered Poulidor, and they were from roughly the same part of France. He had total belief that one day Raymond Poulidor would win the Tour de France for him, and Magne would be celebrated as a Svengali figure. Sadly for them both, the dream was never realized.

Raymond Poulidor at the start of the team time trial stage of the 1966 Tour de France. Mercier-BP finished tenth of 13 teams, but the times only counted for the team classification.

St. Raphaël

1954—1964

St. Raphaël was the first company from outside cycling to be the headline sponsor of a French team. In France, where the cycling federation enforced the rules more zealously, a pretext for St. Raphaël's sponsorship was required. Enter Raphaël Géminiani, the team's lead rider, who helped cook up a ploy to circumvent the rules.

TWO RAPHAËLS

Raphaël Géminiani was a strong rider who in 1955 rode all three Grand Tours in the same year, finishing fourth in the Giro, sixth in the Tour de France, and third in the Vuelta.

The official name for the 1954 team was Saint Raphaël-Raphaël Géminiani. Géminiani, who had just launched an eponymous brand of bike, claimed that the "Saint Raphaël" in the team name referred to him. Many believe that the bike brand was used as a front, to conceal the fact that most of the team's money in 1954, and going forward, came from St. Raphaël, a brand of apéritif containing quinine. In other countries, the team competed as Saint Raphaël-Quinquina, which was the full name of the apéritif. Only in France was the Quinquina reference dropped and Géminiani used in the team name as fairly transparent cover.

The French cycling federation only really took exception to the ruse in 1962, when the Tour de France changed to a trade team formula. Géminiani had stopped racing by then, and was the team's manager. In 1962, he signed the 1957 and 1961 Tour de France winner, Jacques Anquetil, and needed more money to pay for him, so he sold his team to St. Raphaël. The new owner wanted to advertise its brand clearly as the headline sponsor on the team jerseys.

The Tour de France's colorful co-director Jacques Goddet always wore safari-style clothing when in the southern part of France.

The reason Géminiani had used subterfuge before was that the Tour de France directors at the time, Félix Lévitan and Jacques Goddet, were opposed to extra-sportif sponsors. They feared that the involvement of big commercial interests would threaten their control over the sport. Lévitan and Goddet not only ran the Tour

de France like a private dictatorship, they also pulled strings in the wider cycling world, and certainly pulled them in France. Their influence lay behind official suspicion of Géminiani's team while he was racing, and they were certainly behind the wrangles he had with cycling's international body, the UCI (Union Cycliste Internationale), over the registration of the St. Raphaël-Helyett-Hutchinson team over the winter of 1961/1962.

Things weren't resolved at the start of Milan–San Remo on March 19, 1962, when Géminiani told his riders to go to the start line concealing their St. Raphaël jerseys under another one, and to remove the extra jersey as soon as the flag dropped. Things where resolved soon after that incident, and St. Raphaël, with various cosponsors, went on to be one of the best teams ever.

This St. Raphaël-Gitane-Campagnolo jersey is from 1964, the year that Jacques Anquetil won his fifth and final Tour de France.

Rik Van Looy (left) in conversation with Jacques Anquetil during the 1963 Tour de France. Anquetil won the yellow jersey, his fourth victory, and Van Looy won the green.

MAÎTRE JACQUES

Jacques Anquetil is the rider most connected with the St. Raphaël jersey. He won three consecutive Tours de France (1962, 1963, and 1964), the 1963 Vuelta a España, and the 1964 Giro d'Italia for St. Raphaël. Anquetil was also the first rider in history to win the Tour de France five times.

He was a superb time trialist, a fact that underpinned his Grand Tour mastery, but Anquetil could climb with the best if he had to. He had the grim determination to hang on, no matter what the opposition threw at him, if that was what was required to win. He made St. Raphaël a household name,

but he was also an enigma. An undoubted superstar, he and his wife Janine were the glamor couple of 1960s French sport. He was often photographed with pop and movie stars, was reputed to enjoy the finer things of life, and could party hard. But he was also intensely private. He disliked meeting new people, and relied on Janine to be with him at all times when he did. He appeared totally in command of any situation, but was very nervous, and he worried. He was also very superstitious and consulted a clairvoyant before making decisions.

The British connection

St. Raphaël, or rather Saint Raphaël, gave Briton Brian Robinson his first full professional contract in 1957, and Robinson repaid the team's faith by finishing third in Milan-San Remo, the first British rider on the podium of one of the five races known collectively as the Monuments of Cycling.

Robinson understood how pro cycling worked and became a very good team rider, but he could also win, as his victory in the 1961 Critérium du Dauphiné proved. He was also Britain's first stage winner in the Tour de France (he won a stage in the 1958 and 1959 Tours). And he introduced the next notable British rider, Tom Simpson, to the St. Raphaël team. If Brian Robinson opened the doors of professional road racing to British cyclists, Tom Simpson blew them off their hinges. Turning pro for Saint Raphaël in August 1959, Simpson finished fourth in the world road race championships. Of all the British riders to have competed, only he and, more recently, Mark Cavendish have ever finished higher than that.

Simpson then won the Tour du Sud-Est for the team in 1960, and the Tour of Flanders in 1961. But, convinced of his future, Simpson left the team at the end of 1961 because Jacques Anquetil was joining, and Simpson saw himself as a rival to the Frenchman, not a teammate.

The St. Raphaël training top is a lovely piece of knitwear, with timeless style that would sell today.

Pelforth-Sauvage-Lejeune

1962—1968

During the 1960s, Pelforth was an independent brewer from Dunkirk in the north of France. The brand, with the distinctive pelican on the label, continues today as part of the Heineken group.

Pelforth benefitted from the work of Raphaël Géminiani, who pushed to get extra-sportif companies accepted as headline sponsors on team jerseys. In 1961, Pelforth's name was only on the sleeves of the small Sauvage-Lejeune-Pelfort 43 team. Cycling in the 1960s was a blue-collar sport, and it was very popular in northern France, Belgium, and Holland, all regions in which Pelforth could sell its beers.

Sauvage-Lejeune was a bike brand from Paris owned by brothers Roger and Marcel Lejeune. The name Sauvage, French for "savage," came from the somewhat controversial head-badge emblem. The top Sauvage-Lejeune race bikes were red with blue panels, and the Pelforth's beer label colors and logo are predominantly red and yellow. Despite this, there was no red on the Pelforth-Sauvage-Lejeune team jerseys. The top third was yellow with white bands, and there was a wider white chest band. The bottom half was blue.

A modern copy of the Pelforth-Sauvage-Lejeune team jersey from 1966, the one year the top section was solid yellow rather than yellow and white bands.

Four Dutch cyclists at the start of the 1963 Tour de France. The two Pelforth riders are Jan Janssen, far left, and Dick Enthoven.

THE TOP RIDERS

The top Pelforth rider was Jan Janssen, who won the 1964 professional world road race title and in 1968 became the first Dutchman to win the Tour de France. Other notables included the Groussard brothers, Georges and Joseph. Georges was the better stage racer and finished fourth in the 1964 Tour de France, and Joseph won the 1963 Milan–San Remo.

Henri Anglade was another Pelforth star, although his achievements didn't match his considerable promise. He was a very good rider who was unlucky not to have won the 1959 Tour de France, when as a French regional team rider the French national team rode against him (see page 90). He challenged again in the 1960 Tour, wearing the yellow jersey for two days, but faded. After that, Anglade showed flashes of brilliance, such as when he won the 1965 French championships, but he was never consistent.

Pelforth's team manager was Maurice De Muer, one of the best in the business. Long before the days of "marginal gains"— the method of achieving significant improvement in overall performance through small advances in numerous aspects of professional cycling—De Muer often had his riders look at what he thought were key stages in the Tour de France, and would plan meticulously how to ride them. He was a tough taskmaster and known as "The Little Napoleon."

Two British riders raced for Pelforth-Sauvage-Lejeune: Vin Denson for one year in 1963 and Alan Ramsbottom in 1963 and 1964. Ramsbottom was a good rider who didn't get a fair try in European racing. He finished 16th overall in his first Tour de France, but, although he remained with Pelforth, he wasn't selected to race the following year owing to a team dispute. He returned to the UK at the end of 1965.

Kas-Kaskol

1963—1975

This Spanish team was the bane of 1960s and early '70s Grand Tour contenders. It was full of talented climbers who attacked in swarms on mountain climbs. They could not be ignored because, if given any leeway, they would cause devastation. Although the flat stages and time trials were often its riders' undoing, Kas won many races, and, even when they didn't win, they made sure the man who did had sleepless nights and very sore legs.

TARANGU

If any single rider embodied the spirit of Kas-Kaskol, it was José Manuel Fuente. Known in Spain by his nickname, El Tarangu, a word in Asturian meaning "a man of strength and character," Fuente was the perfect climber—short, compact, and without a gram of excess weight, he also possessed a climber's restless spirit and a constant impatience for the road to tip upward so he could attack. Like so many climbers, Fuente lived to attack, and his attacks were so dangerous they even changed the way Eddy Merckx raced.

The Spanish predominantly yellow version of the Kas-Campagnolo team jersey, from the 1976 to 1979 period, when the team started recruiting Belgian as well as Spanish riders.

The 1974 Tour de France podium: Raymond Poulidor (2nd), Eddy Merckx (1st), and Vicente López Carril of the Kas team, who is wearing the Spanish national champion's jersey (3rd).

Fuente joined the Kas team in 1971, won a stage and the King of the Mountains in the Giro d'Italia, then won two stages in the Tour de France. He won the 1972 Vuelta a España, taking at the same time the mountains title and winning one stage. Then he really went after Eddy Merckx in the Giro d'Italia that year, ably supported by his Kas teammates.

"They were all good climbers," says Eddy Merckx. "That was a problem. Fuente was the best, but you could not allow any of them to gain much in the mountains. I think the team had three riders in the top five of the Giro that year. They fought me hard many times, but they gave me the most difficult day on the Blockhaus climb in the 1972 Giro," Merckx said. That stage was

short, from Francavilla al Mare uphill all the way for 30 miles (48 km) to the top of Blockhaus. The climb started in Pretoro, and as the road steepened, Kas attacked. In only 1¼ miles (2 km) they ripped the race to ribbons.

Santiago Lazcano was the first to go, and Merckx, realizing that if he reacted too quickly Kas would take it in turns to attack him, did the only thing he could do. "I went hard, but instead of closing down on Lazcano, which I normally did with any attack, I would try to crush it immediately, I went at a pace I knew I could keep until the top. I decided the thing to do was ride my own race and take my chance with what the Spaniards might gain," Merckx says.

Merckx hammered out a brutal but steady rhythm, fast enough to have the other Kas riders in a line behind him, and enough eventually to bring Lazcano back. In so doing, Merckx drew the sting from all of the Spanish wasps bar one—José Manuel Fuente. He attacked and put 2 minutes 36 seconds into Merckx by the finish to take the race lead. But then Fuente kept on attacking Merckx, and the Belgian kept riding at his own steady but very hard pace. Eventually, Merckx's own attacks and his iron-hard resilience wore Fuente down, and the Spaniard lost the lead and had to settle for second place overall. But he'd taken the fight to Merckx, and kept doing so until his last big victory in the 1974 Vuelta a España, when he also won two stages.

THE JERSEY

The Kas-Kaskol team colors were a yellow torso with blue sleeves, but in most pictures you will see its riders wearing jerseys with a blue torso and yellow sleeves. That's because more pictures are taken during the Tour de France than any other race, and in the Tour de France, Kas's normal team uniform was too close to the Tour's yellow jersey, prompting the Tour organizers to instruct them to change to blue with yellow, instead of the other way around.

It was the same with the Spanish ONCE team in the 1990s, and the Italian squad Mercatone Uno. They both had predominantly yellow jerseys, but they chose to wear pink during the Tour de France. It wasn't a good look.

Kas is a Spanish soft drinks brand, whose owner at the time the Kas-Kaskol team competed, Louis Knorr, was a big cycling fan. He had sponsored small teams since 1958, but the rule change allowing extra-sportif companies to be headline sponsors encouraged him to sponsor a big team. He subsequently took on a full international program of races from 1963 onward. The team changed its name to Kas-Campagnolo from 1976 until 1979, and began recruiting more Belgian riders. Then Kas pulled out of big-team sponsorship until 1985.

Francisco Galdós was one of the many brilliant Spanish climbers in the 1960s and '70s Kas teams. He spent 11 of his 12 pro racing years with the team.

Sean Kelly

Louis Knorr had many friends in cycling, and he kept in touch with them,
even when his company had stepped away from the sport. One of Knorr's best
friends was the French team manager Jean de Gribaldy. During a hunting trip on
Knorr's Basque estate, de Gribaldy talked him into letting his company take over
sponsorship of de Gribaldy's team. Its star rider was Sean Kelly.

The Irishman added to his already astounding success with Kas, winning Milan-
San Remo and Paris-Roubaix in 1986, then narrowly missing out on a Vuelta a
España victory the following year, when he had to retire while leading close
to the end. Kelly made amends in 1988 and won the Vuelta, his only Grand Tour
victory, but that was also the year that Louis Knorr died, and with him no longer
at the helm, Kas pulled out of team sponsorship. However, the company has since
sponsored individual cyclo-cross riders, due to the popularity of the sport in
Vitoria, northern Spain, where Kas is headquartered.

Ireland's Sean Kelly, one of
cycling's major stars, was
the big name in the 1980s
Kas team, when it changed
from a Grand Tour to a
Classics-winning squad.

Bic

1967–1974

After St. Raphaël withdrew from cycling sponsorship, Raphaël Géminiani was tasked with finding new backers for his team. After a successful two-year agreement with Ford, the Bic consumer goods company stepped in to offer sponsorship on a longer-term basis

When St. Raphaël ended its support for Géminiani's team at the end of 1964, Raphaël persuaded the French wing of the Ford Motor Company to take over the team on a two-year contract. Success followed, with a Tour de France victory through

Lucien Aimar in 1966, and an astounding Jacques Anquetil double, when he won the 1965 Critérium du Dauphiné and the longest single-day race, the 365-mile (587-km) Bordeaux–Paris, back to back, hardly sleeping between the two.

ONE-BRAND TEAM

Bic was the first extra-sportif sponsor to commit to almost the entire budget of running a team. It had bike suppliers—Jacques Anquetil-branded bikes were the first, and Motobécane followed later—and tire and equipment suppliers, but Bic was the only name on the jerseys.

Bic was founded in 1945 by Marcel Bich, who inherited the title Baron Bich from his father. He had worked in the printing trade and the first products Bic made were fountain pens. In 1950, Bich bought the patent for the ballpoint pen from a Hungarian, Lázlo Biró, and transferred production to Paris.

The Bic team, clad in the company's predominantly orange kit, won some races in the late sixties, but the great Anquetil was at the end of his career. The team signed the 1968 Tour de France winner Jan Janssen in 1969, the year of Anquetil's retirement, but Janssen underperformed. It wasn't until Bic signed a young Spaniard called Luis Ocaña

A Bic jersey from early on in the team's history. The design changed very little, but the front pockets were abandoned on most cycling jerseys by 1970.

From left to right: Jacques Anquetil, Jan Janssen, and Raymond Poulidor at a track meeting shortly after the 1968 Tour de France, which Janssen won.

in 1970 that things really improved. By then, Maurice De Muer ran the team, and, with a much larger budget than he had had with Pelforth-Sauvage-Lejeune, he set about building a team to support the incredible talent he had seen in Ocaña. Within a year Roger Rosiers had won Paris–Roubaix for Bic, and Luis Ocaña was challenging Eddy Merckx. He humbled Merckx in the Alps during the 1971 Tour de France, taking the yellow jersey by many minutes only to crash out in the Pyrenees. Ocaña wasn't so good the following year, but with Merckx missing the race, Ocaña tore the 1973 Tour de France field apart.

De Muer had his team ride hard over a cobbled stage in the north in the first week, giving Ocaña a time cushion over his rivals before the first mountain was reached. Then Ocaña dominated in the Alps and Pyrenees, winning six stages in all, and the overall classification by over 15 minutes.

Sadly Ocaña was never as good again, and Bic had received the publicity it needed from cycling through the 1973 Tour win, so it pulled out of the sport at the end of 1974. However, Bic made a return to cycling in 2012 as a sponsor of the Tour de France.

Salvarani

1963–1972

An Italian manufacturer of kitchen equipment, Salvarani represented Italian sixties chic in its kitchens and in its cycling jersey. The jersey was very modern, a block of blue with just the logos added—no bands, no contrasting sleeves, just perfect blue Italian style, enhanced toward the end of the decade when Bianchi became Salvarani's bike supplier.

HUMBLE BEGINNINGS

The Salvarani team jersey was a lesson in conveying what a brand is about. It is simple, elegant, and it fitted in perfectly with Salvarani's overall marketing effort.

Salvarani wasn't a big team in 1963; Arnaldo Pambianco was the best rider, and he won a stage in the Giro d'Italia but not much else. The team was strengthened the following year when the elegant Vittorio Adorni and tough Vito Taccone joined, but 1965 would be the big year for Salvarani. Adorni won the Giro d'Italia, and a new signing, the 22-year-old Felice Gimondi, winner of the previous year's amateur Tour de France and the Tour de l'Avenir, won the pro Tour. Gimondi took the yellow jersey early and then lost it, and was expected to fall back. Instead, he got stronger and stronger, and won. Gimondi also won the 1966 Paris–Roubaix and Il Lombardia, and he won the Giro d'Italia twice for Salvarani, in 1967 and 1969.

Salvarani has the same logo today as it had on its cycling jersey in the 1960s and '70s. It is a design classic, with the logo colors, black and red, reflected in the collar and cuffs. Its design was inspired by Italian manufacturing icons such as Vespa and Fiat, and the company was very progressive. It not only sponsored a cycling team but sponsored the 1965 Beatles concert in Milan, and many other events.

Gimondi won the 1967 Giro d'Italia for Salvarani. It was the 80th edition of the race. He's doing a lap of honor around the Arena Civica in Milan with the rest of his team.

The Salvarani cycling team would have had a British connection had it not been for the tragic death of Tom Simpson from heart failure, caused by dehydration, on Mont Ventoux during the 1967 Tour de France. Simpson had wanted out from his French team Peugeot for a while, but Peugeot insisted he sign his contract for the following year before the current year's Tour de France, the inference being that if he didn't sign, Peugeot wouldn't pick him for the Tour. That would have been bad news. Riders in the 1960s needed the Tour not only as a shop window, as they do now; they also needed it to gain entry to the lucrative post-Tour critérium races. No Tour meant no critérium contracts, which meant a lot less money for the year.

That changed for Simpson in 1967 when the Tour de France reverted back to national teams. With an automatic place in the British team, Simpson signed for Salvarani. He had built up a good friendship with Felice Gimondi, and they were to share leadership of the team. Simpson was even afforded the luxury of bringing fellow Brit Vin Denson to the team as a domestique. It would have been a good move for all concerned, but sadly it never happened.

Flandria

1959–1970

Flandria was a Flemish cycling institution. Flanders considers cycling to be a part of its identity—this region of Belgium has produced more champions, more winners of big bike races, than any comparably sized area in the world. Cycling matters in Flanders, and for a long time Flandria was its national team.

Leon Vandaele, facing the camera, waiting for the start of the 1959 Paris-Roubaix, surrounded by Dr. Mann-Flandria teammates.

Flandria was a bike and motorbike manufacturer based in West Flanders. It was owned by the Claeys family and run by two brothers, Aimé and Remi Claeys, until they split and Remi set up rival brand Superia. Flandria made a wide range of bikes, and its best race models were painted bright red, with white panels on the seat tube and down tube, and Flandria decals in lowercase letters over the panels.

The rainbow bands on this Flandria-Velda jersey show it was for the end 1977 races, when Freddy Maertens no longer had the rainbow jersey he had won in previous years.

STEPPING ON TOES

Aimé Claeys liked bike racing, and he helped a few local amateurs and independent pro racers by supplying bikes, but in 1959, when he was looking to expand his race bike production, a chance meeting helped him make a decision that would have a huge effect on international cycling. Claeys was in a café one Sunday morning when a local pro racer, Leon Vandaele, dropped in. Vandaele was good, a very fast sprinter, but he found himself without a team because he hadn't obeyed team orders. He had been in the Faema-Guerra team, led by Rik Van Looy, with a roster of riders intended to support Van Looy. Vandaele, however, refused to do that. He had won the 1958 Paris–Roubaix, and felt he was ready to challenge for

victory in other high-profile events. Van Looy didn't agree, and Vandaele found himself out of the team.

Claeys liked Vandaele, so together with a cosponsor, Dr. Mann, he built a team around Vandaele for the 1959 racing season, and he persuaded the legendary Flemish racer Briek Schotte to be its rider and manager. The team won 44 races, with Vandaele taking eight victories, including Ghent–Wevelgem. The following year, Schotte became the full-time manager, and the team grew. It really hit the big time in 1962, when, ironically, Rik Van Looy joined, bringing Faema with him as a cosponsor. The team won 101 races that year, and was the UCI team world cup winner.

All through the 1960s, Flandria was one of the best three teams in Belgium, along with Wiel's-Groene Leeuw and Solo-Superia, but when the latter two teams stopped, Flandria became the sole standard-bearer for Flemish cycling. By then, Eddy Merckx was lead rider for an Italian team, which was built the way Van Looy built his teams, everybody riding for the leader. But Flandria had the talented De Vlaeminck brothers, Walter Godefroot, Jean-Pierre Monseré, and Eric Leman, then later Freddy Maertens, all of them capable of winning big races, and they fought Merckx all the way. But Flandria hit financial difficulties toward the end of the 1970s and pulled out of sponsorship.

The Flandria team line up at the start of the 1964 Tour de France. The team manager, far right, is Guillaume Driessens, who would go on to manage Eddy Merckx.

THE JERSEY

Flandria joined with a number of cosponsors over the years, who were represented to varying extents on the team's jersey, but the jersey's basic pattern was always the same—fiery red with a white chest band and a white band on each sleeve. The team's bikes were the same shade of red, with white panels.

The Flandria team became known as the Red Devils. In 1962, for one year when Rik Van Looy joined the team, bringing his Italian sponsor Faema with him, it became part of Rik's Red Guard (see page 157). Flandria's best years were the late 1960s and '70s, when they became the epicenter of Flemish talent, and they really took the battle to Eddy Merckx. Merckx is the greatest cyclist ever, but for a while, in certain races, Flandria riders had the beating of him.

Eric de Vlaeminck leading Eddy Merckx in the 1970 Amstel Gold Race in Holland. It was won by another Belgian, Georges Pintens, who can just be seen behind De Vlaeminck.

The Bulldog bites the Cannibal

Eddy Merckx won nearly every race in cycling, and most of them many times—his hunger for victory was so great he was called the Cannibal. Desipte his dominance, he has always paid tribute to one man, Walter Godefroot (nicknamed the Bulldog), whom Merckx says, "is the only one of my adversaries I never beat in a direct fight for victory." Godefroot was a Flandria rider.

Actually Merckx's quote flatters Godefroot. He was never a mountain climber, so never in direct conflict with Merckx in the Grand Tours, but in the late '60s Classics, Godefroot inflicted three comprehensive defeats on Merckx. The first was Liège-Bastogne-Liège in 1967, the second the Tour of Flanders in 1968, and the third, Godefroot's greatest win, was Paris-Roubaix in 1969. Merckx had totally dominated the 1969 season to that point, obliterating everyone in the Tour of Flanders one week before. But Godefroot was determined to beat Merckx, especially when he had two teammates, Roger and Erik De Vlaeminck, in the front group with him, so he started attacking.

His third attack was a classic Roubaix attack—he hit it hard coming off a cobbled sector. The rest of his group hesitated for a moment, and Godefroot quickly put 50 yards (45 meters) into them. His first two attacks had thinned down the field, but they were softening-up blows; this was for real. This was for the race.

Godefroot piled on the pressure. He didn't look round to see if Merckx was gaining. That would have been a waste. He just pounded a huge gear with his mouth wide open, his chest heaving, and his eyes fixed resolutely ahead. This was real bulldog stuff. Godefroot had the race between his teeth and wouldn't let go. There were 17 miles (28 km) left. Merckx tried, but that day he couldn't stop Godefroot winning for Flandria, and for Flanders.

Solo-Superia

1964-1966

Solo, a Belgian margarine brand, entered cycling in 1961 to sponsor a team that included the great Rik Van Steenbergen, one of the best all-round racers there has ever been. But Van Steenbergen was almost 40 years old by then, and he had been a pro for nearly 20 years. In 1964, Solo joined the bike manufacturer Superia in sponsoring a new team built around Rik Van Looy. Solo-Superia became the next chapter in the story of Rik's Red Guard.

Rik Van Looy with the rest of the Solo-Superia team in 1964. He's wearing a different jersey to them because he was Belgian champion at the time.

Ward Sels, a key member of the "Red Guard," was a rider whom Van Looy saw as a possible successor. However, injuries sustained in a bad crash eventually curtailed his career.

There were two ways this could be achieved. The first was to use crosswinds in races to create an echelon at the front into which only Van Looy and his teammates were allowed. Strong teams like Etixx-Quick Step still do it today. The first rider in the diagonal echelon rides just far enough out in the road for his team to get shelter. The other riders either hang on behind and hope the course changes direction, or they form a similar echelon behind. If the latter happens, the race hinges on which echelon is strongest.

The other way Van Looy's teams could engineer victory for him was by leading him out in a sprint. He was a formidable sprinter anyway, but he worked out that if his teammates set the pace for him he could exert control on the peloton. This was instead of it being a free-for-all, in which he could get baulked or boxed in. Van Looy's teams invented the lead-out train in sprints.

The first team Van Looy created was sponsored by the Italian coffee machine manufacturer Faema, and its jersey was mainly red. So as Van Looy's victory list grew, and as cycling saw the imperial manner in which he led his team, he became known as the Emperor, and his team was called the Red Guard.

THE RED GUARD

Rik Van Looy is one of the all-time greats. He is the only rider to have won every Classic, the Classics being the collective name for the five Monuments of Cycling, plus a select number of other big single-day races. Soon after he started winning the races in 1956, Van Looy developed a template that would ensure him more victories. For it to work, though, he needed a team that was totally dedicated to him, and that would work together to engineer victories for him.

The Solo-Superia jersey made famous by Rik's Red Guard. The British pro Vin Denson, who rode for the team in 1964, described them as "a bunch of cut-throat thugs."

THE JERSEY

It was blood-red with a black band around each sleeve and around the neck. The writing was embroidered in white cotton, and the team were issued with jerseys with both front and back pockets and, as was becoming the fashion, jerseys with back pockets only. Superia, the bike sponsor, was a bike brand created by Remi Claeys, after he had split from his brother Aimé and their company Flandria. However, the split didn't require Remi to move to a new location. With typical Flemish practicality, Aimé and Remi simply built a dividing wall down the middle of the Flandria factory, and each kept to their allotted side.

EDDY'S EXPERIENCE

Solo-Superia was the team Eddy Merckx turned pro for in 1965, but it wasn't a happy experience. Rik Van Looy didn't like him. He viewed Merckx as a soft young man from a middle-class area of Brussels, who had had everything handed to him on a plate, in stark contrast to the opinion he had of himself as a self-made man who had had to work hard for all he had achieved.

Van Looy quickly saw that Merckx was easily embarrassed, and he took delight in embarrassing him. He criticized what he ate, and how he ate it. He criticized the young man's appearance. He criticized everything and, anxious to please their boss, the rest of the team did the same. Merckx thinks now that Van Looy should have been easier on him, because he was young and finding his confidence. Van Looy just thinks Merckx couldn't take a joke.

Solo-Superia made life difficult for Merckx. His first race was Flèche Wallonne, a Classic. He punctured early and had to chase back alone because nobody from his team dropped back to help him. Merckx wound up exhausted, and pulled out of the race at three-quarter distance. But Merckx was too good to hold back. Three weeks later, on May 11, 1965, he won his first pro race, and from that point Merckx got better and better. He won six races between May 11 and August 1, when the Belgian National Championships was held. By then he was a thorn in Rik Van Looy's side. The kid might have been soft but he was good, and even though Van Looy was the defending national champion, he did nothing when a breakaway containing another young rider, one in a rival team, went ahead.

The rider was Walter Godefroot, and Van Looy makes no secret even today that he preferred Godefroot to Merckx. Godefroot took the bronze medal in the 1964 Olympic road race in Tokyo, and was tipped for stardom alongside Eddy. "Godefroot was more like me, both as a rider and in his personality. He wasn't easily wound up all the time like Eddy Merckx was," Van Looy says.

When Godefroot's breakaway had a good lead, Van Looy quit the race. His team lost interest and Merckx had to chase alone to catch Godefroot, who had his teammate and brother-in-law Arthur Decabooter with him. The two teammates then attacked Merckx in turn, forcing him to chase, until Godefroot, who was a faster sprinter anyway, beat Merckx to the line, with Decabooter in third place.

Van Looy and Merckx hardly spoke after that, and Merckx signed for the Peugeot team for 1966 and 1967, where his talent was nurtured and valued. Even now, so many years later, Eddy Merckx and Rik Van Looy aren't friends.

Walter Godefroot winning the final stage of the Tour de France on July 20, 1975, the first ever to finish on the Champs-Élysées.

Wiel's-Groene Leeuw

1962-1966

Groene Leeuw, "green lion" in Flemish, was a Belgian bike manufacturer that sponsored teams on its own from 1945 until 1961. Wiel's was a Belgian brewer specializing in low-alcohol beers. Wiel's-Groene Leeuw favored riders from East Flanders, where Groene Leeuw was based, while Flandria favored West Flandrians, where Flandria was based. For a while their rivalry was a nice little subplot to the ever-present battle between Flanders and the French-speaking part of Belgium.

The Wiel's-Groene Leeuw jersey was predominantly dark green, traditionally the color Groene Leeuw painted its bikes, with a red chest band for the Wiel's logo. On the genuine pro team jerseys Groene Leeuw was embroidered in gold cotton, although you may see some pictures where it is white.

The team from cycling-mad East Flanders was another with a British member, Michael Wright, who was born in Hertfordshire but has lived almost all his life in Belgium.

The trend of having East Flandrians in the team came from Groene Leeuw, the headquarters of which was in Deinze, just south of Ghent. Benoni Beheyt, a Wiel's-Groene Leeuw rider for his entire career, is from nearby Zwijnaarde. He enjoyed a glittering start to his career but things quickly went wrong after he won the world road race title in 1963.

Beheyt was another rider who fell out with Rik Van Looy, but for reasons other than that the Emperor had taken a dislike to him, as had happened with Eddy Merckx. The root cause, instead, was the finish of the 1963 world championships. Van Looy was on a hat trick of world titles, and Beheyt, who was part of the Belgian team, was vying with him for victory, alongside 50 other riders who sprinted it out for the title. Van Looy wanted to win, of course, but Beheyt was a fast sprinter too, and he wasn't part of Rik's Red Guard. Van Looy asked Beheyt to lead him out, but he refused.

They both hit the front just before the line, then Beheyt reached out and took hold of the back of Van Looy's jersey. Immediately afterward he told reporters that Van Looy was squeezing him up against the barriers, and he reached out to fend him off. Van Looy said Beheyt pulled him backward. Beheyt won, and Van Looy was second.

Beheyt flatly refuses to talk about it now, but Van Looy still says he was pulled back. Beheyt won races the following year, and he made his rainbow jersey look good with second place in the 1964 Paris–Roubaix, but his career quickly dwindled after that, and he stopped racing at the end of 1965. It didn't pay to cross Rik Van Looy.

Wiel's-Groene Leeuw continued its "local team for local riders" policy, when it signed brothers-in-law Arthur Decabooter and Walter Godefroot in 1965. Godefroot was from Deinze, East Flanders, and he won the Belgian championship for the team in his first year. But cycling was growing, and teams needed to be less parochial to flourish. Wiel's pulled out of team sponsorship in 1966 and Groene Leeuw did the same at the end of 1969.

Benoni Beheyt in the rainbow jersey he won as world professional road race champion in 1963.

Period features

In the 1940s, manufacturers experimented by adding synthetic fibers to wool jerseys to get a better, more consistent shape. The synthetic material they used, Rhovyl, which was developed during the 1940s, contains polyvinyl chloride. The name is taken from the developers, Rhône-Poulenc, and the word vinyl. An all-Rhovyl yellow jersey was used for the 1947 Tour de France, but the Frenchman Louison Bobet refused to wear it because he said it made him sweat too much. The Tour went back to wool jerseys after that, but reintroduced wool-Rhovyl mixes later.

Faema

1968–1970

The Italian coffee machine manufacturer Faema had sponsored teams before, and would go on to sponsor again, but always with cosponsors. This team was special because Faema sponsored it alone, and while other Faema teams had good riders in them, this one had the best. This Faema team was the Faema team of Eddy Merckx.

From left to right: Felice Gimondi and Gianni Motta, and two Faema riders, Vittorio Adorni and Eddy Merckx, at the 1968 Giro d'Italia, which Merckx won.

MODERN TEAM

Faema hired a business specialist with a keen interest in cycling to put its 1968 team together. His name was Vincenzo Giacotto, and he wanted to build the team round Eddy Merckx. It would be a modern team.

Giacotto was the general manager, leaving Mario Vigna and Fiorenzo Magni just to get on with the racing. That was a new template for cycling. Previously sports directors had done everything. They directed riders in

races, planned strategy, and with the help
of a secretary did all the team logistics.
Giacotto handled the logistics for Faema,
leaving Vigna and Magni to direct the races.

Giacotto approached Merckx's personal
manager, Jean Van Buggenhout, and hinted
that Faema had money. That interested
Van Buggenhout, who was a canny
operator. He negotiated a three-year deal
for Merckx to ride for Faema at 400,000
Belgian francs a year. That's about $6000,
at a time when a skilled worker in Belgium
earned the equivalent of between $700
and $900 a year. Van Buggenhout also
wanted other Belgians, whom he picked,
to be in the team.

Giacotto agreed, so the 1968 Faema
team had 16 Italians and nine Belgians.
The Belgians included Jos Spruyt, Roger
Swerts, Victor Van Schil, and Martin
Van Den Bossche, who became the core
of an Eddy Merckx superteam. Merckx's
friend and the 1967 world professional
track sprint champion Patrick Sercu was
another Faema rider. But the key man for
Merckx's development was an Italian,
Vittorio Adorni.

KNOCKING THE EDGES OFF

Giacotto thought Merckx could become
one of the greatest cyclists ever, but he
had edges, and they needed knocking off.
Merckx was as strong as a horse, but he
wasn't as light as he could be, and that
would limit him in the mountains. Also,
he was a daredevil descender but his
technique didn't match his ambition.
Merckx descents were a succession of
rushes, squealing brakes and locked
wheels before 1968. He had to improve
his training and his technique.

Eddy Merckx in the Faema
team jersey. The rainbow
bands around his collar and
cuffs denote his 1967 world
professional road race title.

Vittorio Adorni knew how to train and
was a master of technique. He also knew
how to prepare by eating the right things
to support his training. Adorni was 30 and
his career was far from over, as he proved
later in 1968, when he won the world road
race championship, but Giacotto wanted
Adorni to show Eddy Merckx the
subtleties of cycling—subtleties that would
give Merckx the last percentage points he
needed to be truly great.

The work started in January 1968,
when Eddy Merckx attended his first-ever
training camp. By the end of it he had
reduced his racing weight from 165 to
160 pounds (75 to 72 kg), and, as well as
climbing better, Merckx was now a
master of descents.

The distinctive red V-top of the Faema jersey, and Eddy Merckx in the yellow jersey of his first Tour de France in 1969.

THE JERSEY

The 1968 and 1969 Faema jersey was white with a red V-shaped upper section. The sleeves were red too. There was no other lettering on the jersey but the Faema name, which was embroidered in a custom font that the company still uses.

Red is Faema's color. Its earlier teams had predominantly red jerseys, and later in the 1970s, when Faema briefly cosponsored the Bianchi team, its name on the Bianchi celeste jersey had a red background. Faema's tracksuits, a reversal of the racing jerseys, were red with a V-shaped white upper sector. Faema had dark chestnut-brown training tops, and the riders got team-issue leisure gear, which was a first for any team.

In 1970, the third and final year of Merckx's contract with Faema, the jersey design stayed the same but the team's name was changed to Faemino, which was a brand of instant coffee Faema launched that year.

Merckx's Faema and Faemino race jerseys all had the rainbow bands on the collars and cuffs to mark his 1967 world road race title. Of course, when he started his first year with the Faema team, Merckx had the rainbow jersey, which the company kept simple with just the Faema name on the chest and back.

Birth of a bike brand

The 1968 Faema team bikes were made by a Belgian frame builder called Kessels, who was based in Ostend. The frames were white with a red head and seat tube panel, and branded Faema. When he rode for Peugeot, Merckx, like the team leader Tom Simpson, had some frames built by Masi in Milan, but they were sprayed white and Peugeot's name was on them. It was Van Buggenhout who knew Kessels, and he knew he had high standards.

In 1969, the Faema team frames had the same color scheme but were branded Eddy Merckx. They were still made by Kessels, who was later allowed to sell Eddy Merckx-branded bikes to the public. The Faemino team rode Eddy Merckx-branded bikes in 1970, and the decal used with his name on was exactly like the one Merckx used when he started manufacturing bikes in his own factory after he stopped racing. However, the Eddy Merckx brand was actually born when Kessels, and later Falcon Cycles in the UK, began producing Eddy Merckx bikes to sell to the public, because Merckx got a royalty on each one sold.

The iconic lines of the late '60s Faema jersey, made unforgettable thanks to its association with Eddy Merckx.

The other special jersey Merckx raced in was when the team's name changed to Faemino. It was the Belgian champion's jersey, which Merckx won in June 1970. The team kept advertising minimal on that too. In fact all the team's jerseys reflected the understated style of Italian design that is seen in the company's commercial coffee machines today.

A transitional picture. Jacques Anquetil (far left) and Rik Van Looy (far right) are the older generation, whose time in cycling is nearly done. Eddy Merckx (2nd right) and Charly Grosskost (in the white jersey) are part of the new generation. Raymond Poulidor (second left) spans the two.

THE 1970s—A DECADE OF TRANSITION

There were some subtle changes in jersey design during the 1970s, especially toward the end of the decade—a period of change that would quickly gather momentum in the next decade. The '70s also gave us some classic jerseys, like Eddy Merckx's Molteni, Roger De Vlaeminck's Brooklyn, and the TI-Raleigh team's very modern design.

Molteni-Arcore

1958-1976

Molteni was an Italian team sponsored by a salami manufacturer from Arcore, just outside Milan. It is most famous for the period when Eddy Merckx raced for the team, but it had some very good riders and significant victories before his arrival in 1971. Still, it was Eddy Merckx who made Molteni's name known everywhere. So now, through the filter of history, Molteni means Eddy Merckx.

BEST MAN, BEST TEAM

Jean Van Buggenhout negotiated the contracts for Merckx and his Belgian teammates with the Molteni team. He was a trained accountant, and he was tough, intelligent, and very streetwise. Merckx says their relationship was "Always strictly business, and it suited me better that way. I found out how important he was when Van Buggenhout died suddenly in 1974, and I had to run my own business affairs."

Rudi Altig (right) and his older brother Willi. In this shot Rudi is wearing the yellow jersey of the 1966 Tour de France, which he held for ten days after winning stage one.

The 1971 Molteni team was very strong, but Merckx and Van Buggenhout took every opportunity to add to it—not just buying good support riders, but buying some who could have been rivals. Barry Hoban raced against Eddy Merckx through his whole career, and he says. "He was the greatest, there is no doubt about it, but what many people don't realise is that Merckx also had the greatest team.

"They'd split the race up for him by forming echelons in crosswinds, just like Rik Van Looy's team did. He had strong climbers to set a high pace in the mountains to stop the other climbers attacking. He'd have riders who could get in breaks with him, and work to get them established. Then if you were there and he attacked alone he'd still have riders strong enough in the chasing group to get in the way of your efforts to catch him.

"Don't get me wrong, Eddy would have still won as much if he hadn't had such a super strong team, but he wouldn't have won by the margins he did. He asked me to join Molteni once. The money was good, but I didn't want to spend every race working for Eddy Merckx to win. I wanted to win some myself."

This pre-Eddy Merckx Molteni-Acore team jersey is another example of Italian restraint and style.

THE JERSEY

The pre-1971 Molteni team colors were brown with a dark blue chest band. Big winners for Molteni during that period were the German 1966 world road race champion Rudi Altig, the 1966 Giro d'Italia winner Gianni Motta, and the 1970 Milan–San Remo winner Michele Dancelli. When Merckx and his Belgian teammates joined in 1971 the colors changed slightly and the brown became more of an orange brown, which Merckx called "Pumpkin," saying, "I know its name because it was to match the color of the paint of the team bikes."

The Molteni team bikes were made by Ernesto Colnago until Eddy Merckx set a new Hour Record in 1972. Colnago wanted to publicize the fact that he'd built the bike, which was a technological masterpiece for its day, but Jean Van Buggenhout wouldn't allow him to. Their relationship ended, and Colnago started producing the Colnago Mexico series of bikes, with no reference to Merckx, and they really established Colnago as a stand-alone brand. Ugo De Rosa took over making bikes for Eddy Merckx and the rest of the Molteni team. The jerseys remained pumpkin and deep blue, with Molteni on the chest band, back, and sleeves, and the word "Arcore," where Molteni salami was produced, on the front. This lasted until Molteni pulled out of pro team sponsorship at the end of 1976.

Eddy Merckx shakes hands with Dutchman, Joop Zoetemelk, who was one of his closest and regular rivals, at a race in Holland in August 1973.

THE CURIOUS CASE OF MARTIN VAN DEN BOSSCHE

Martin Van Den Bossche was an ungainly cyclist. Tall and gawky, he rode with his elbows stuck out, chose the weirdest gear combinations, and often rode with the chain on the bike's inner chainring and smallest sprockets. But he could fly. He was one of the strong Belgians Jean Van Buggenhout contracted to help Merckx in the Faema team, and he did help, especially on the epic stage 17 in the Pyrenees in the 1969 Tour, when Merckx doubled his overall lead.

The Tourmalet, the third of four mountain passes that day, is a climb that every rider dreams of crossing in the lead. Van Den Bossche set the pace for Merckx up the Tourmalet, stringing everybody out behind him, but as they neared the top he asked Merckx if he could lead over the climb. He'd paced Merckx up the Peyresourde, the Aspin, and now the Tourmalet, so it was a quite normal and reasonable request. But Merckx refused, and is quoted as saying, "Martin, I'm the boss, I go over first." To which it is said that Van Den Bossche replied, "Well, you can ride to the finish on your own then." And he stopped working. Merckx did ride to the finish on his own; he attacked near the top of the Tourmalet, went over the summit alone in the lead, and flew down the other side. And he carried on alone for the rest of the stage, extending his overall lead from 8 to a massive 16 minutes.

Van Den Bossche was fed up with riding for Eddy Merckx. He didn't mind working for him but wanted some crumbs of glory. He also says, "Eddy got on my nerves with his constant competitiveness. He had to win everything, including things outside of cycling. We played in a charity football match once, and I let in a goal on purpose, just to see what he'd do. Merckx went crazy. I thought that was really odd."

Anyway, Van Den Bossche decided he'd had enough of Merckx and signed for Molteni during the 1969 Tour de France. But he only got one year of freedom, because Merckx joined Molteni in 1971 and Van Den Bossche got stuck with his old job of driving the Merckx train through the mountains again.

Eddy Merckx and Molteni. This shot is from the 1971 Tour de France; in later editions of the team, the jersey lightened until it was closer to the color of the team bikes.

Gitane-Campagnolo

1975-1977

Gitane is a French bike manufacturer with a long history of sponsorship. It had scored many victories, including two Tours de France, before it linked up with Campagnolo. Gitane went on to combine with Renault and dominate the Tour de France, winning six out of the seven Tours between 1978 and 1984. Gitane-Campagnolo was a transition between those two eras, but in its short life the team still won the Tour de France and several other big races.

TEAM HISTORY

Gitane was the bike supplier to St. Raphaël when Jacques Anquetil won the 1963 and 1964 Tours de France. The company took on a team in its own right in 1972 and 1973. In 1974 it merged with the Sonolor TV team to become Sonolor-Gitane. In 1975 it was Gitane-Campagnolo.

The team manager was the former racer and right-hand man of Jacques Anquetil, Jean Stablinski. He was a master tactician. Not particularly brilliant in the physical aspect of cycling, Stablinski built a great career through his personal racing philosophy:

Jean Stablinski, a tactical powerhouse and no mean racer. Stablinski won the Vuelta a España in 1958 and was world road race champion in 1962.

Bernard Hinault won the 1978 Tour de France on a Gitane bike, when the team's headline sponsor was Renault. It was the first of five Tour victories for the Frenchman.

"If you aren't the strongest in any racing situation, you have to be the craftiest." He was joined in 1975 by Cyrille Guimard, a good rider whose career had ended prematurely through injury. Guimard still had a pro cyclist's fierce will to win, and he learned a lot from the crafty Stablinski.

The team also made two important rider signings in 1975. One was the Belgian climber Lucien Van Impe, who had already achieved a Tour de France podium place and two King of the Mountains titles. The other was a 20-year-old rookie professional from Brittany called Bernard Hinault. They would both prove a great investment. The Van Impe call paid off immediately; he won his third Tour de France King of the Mountains title in 1975. That was the first year that the polka-dot jersey was awarded to the leader of the competition. The following year he would do even better.

Hinault was more of a long-term investment, and under the guidance of Cyrille Guimard, who made Hinault his personal project, the rookie's undoubted talent was nurtured and developed slowly, which helped ensure it would last. Guimard wouldn't let Hinault ride the Tour de France for his first three years with the team, but when he won Ghent–Wevelgem, Liège–Bastogne–Liège, and the Critérium du Dauphiné in 1977, Guimard knew he was ready for the Tour de France in 1978.

THE JERSEY

The Gitane-Campagnolo jersey employed a complicated design. The red and yellow bands that ran across the shoulders were carried across from the earlier Sonolor-Gitane design. There was a white chest band, with "Gitane" and "Campagnolo" emblazoned across it, and the lower segment was blue with a band of interlocking white circles. The sleeves were white and the collars and cuffs red.

One thing to notice with pro team jerseys from the mid-1970s onward is the way their lettering changed. Expensive embroidery was slowly replaced by flocked lettering, which was ironed onto the blank jerseys. It was quick and cheap, and looked good when the jerseys were new, but flocked lettering tends to fade, so that many originals from this era don't look so good now.

The Gitane-Campagnolo jersey had so many echoes of previous teams it ended up looking like what it was—a mix of ideas.

Lucien Van Impe (right), the first winner of the polka-dot jersey in the Tour de France. His teammate Willy Teirlinck was Belgian national champion in 1975.

When Van Impe attacked, the other race favorite, Joop Zoetemelk, who was going well, didn't react. Luis Ocaña went with Van Impe, but Ocaña had lost time early on so was no threat overall, and being a good time trialist, he was a big help to Van Impe between the climbs. The pair of them steadily gained time until the foot of Pla d'Adet, where Van Impe surged ahead and kept surging all the way to the top to take the yellow jersey by over three minutes from Zoetemelk. By Paris, he had extended his lead to over four.

Cyrille Guimard has always claimed he had to bully Van Impe into attacking on that stage, but Van Impe's recollection is different: "Guimard didn't order me to attack, because I didn't attack, it was just a case of accelerating steadily throughout the stage. First I chased to get in a group with Luis Ocaña and a few others at the front, while Joop Zoetemelk, my main rival, stayed in the group behind watching the yellow jersey, Raymond Delisle.

"Once in the front group, I increased my effort and was soon alone. I figured that Zoetemelk was playing to his nature, watching the yellow jersey, then he would attack late in the stage and try and get time on Delisle. He was discounting me, and that was my chance. So I turned up the effort even more, despite the fact that there was a long way to go. Eventually Guimard did come up to me in the team car, but all it was for was to give me an update on Zoetemelk. By that time I was gone," Van Impe says.

VAN IMPE'S TOUR

"Cyrille Guimard and I went to the 1976 Tour de France presentation together in October 1975, and straightaway I could see that they had made the 1976 race a tough one. They had designed it for Bernard Thévenet, a good climber. But what was designed for Thévenet was also designed for me. I said right there at the presentation that I wasn't going for the King of the Mountains or for the stages, I was going for victory," Lucien Van Impe remembers. He won the 1976 Tour in the way only a true climber can win, with one glorious attack in the mountains. It was on stage 14, Saint-Gaudens to Saint-Lary-Soulan, with the climbs of the Portillon, Peyresourde, and the very difficult Pla d'Adet to finish on.

Fiat

1977–1978

He's close to the end of his career and some of his strength has gone, but the style is still there. Eddy Merckx takes a corner in the Fiat team kit.

Fiat was brought into cycling by Eddy Merckx. Molteni's withdrawal from sponsorship at the end of 1976 was a shock, but Merckx heard that Fiat was thinking about getting involved in cycling so he persuaded the Italian car company to take on the riders Merckx wanted from Molteni, plus a few others, on a one-year contract. However, Merckx was past his best, and the contract wasn't renewed. Fiat carried on in 1978, sponsoring a young team, but it lasted only a year.

A SENSE OF DUTY

The Fiat jerseys was a classic interpretation of the company's blue and white colors. Merckx had a contract with Adidas for the previous couple of years, so just like the 1975 and 1976 Molteni jersey, the 1977 Fiat jerseys had Adidas's three white bands on the shoulders.

Merckx trained hard over the preceding winter and won his first race in 1977, the GP Aix-en-Provence, but the back trouble that started after a terrible crash in 1969 had flared up considerably during the second half of 1975 and all of 1976, growing ever worse. "Sometimes it felt like I was only pedaling with one leg," he says now. Merckx rode a defiant Tour de France to finish sixth, but the photos show he suffered terribly to do it. Merckx says now, "I made a mistake at the end of my career, but I made it for the right reason. I owed a debt of support to my team because of all the work they had done for me over the years. When I got punched and lost the lead in the 1975 Tour, and especially when I fell and fractured my cheek, I should have stopped. But I didn't because my team would have lost potential prize money for my second place overall. I carried on, but dug really deep to do so, and I was never the same again," he says.

In contrast to Gitane-Campagnolo, the Fiat jersey was a perfect representation of the team's sponsor, which is what all good pro cycling jerseys are.

That sense of duty—Merckx and some of his team had been together since 1968—was why Merckx tried to race in 1978. He negotiated a deal for most of his Fiat riders to join a new team sponsored by the clothing chain C&A, but during a race in Belgium, the Circuit of Waasland, in which he finished sixth, Merckx decided enough was enough and he never raced again.

The 1978 Fiat team, which was hastily cobbled together by a new manager, Raphaël Géminiani, was full of young, inexperienced riders, some of whom went on to have quite successful careers. One of them was Britain's Paul Sherwen. "It was certainly an adventure, I'll say that for Fiat. Working with Géminiani had never a dull moment either. He had some funny views. For example, he never bought us rain tops. He just said, 'You can't race with your coat on.' I think we won one race, early on in the Tour of the Mediterranean," Sherwen remembers.

Brooklyn

1973-1977

This is either the classiest or most garish of 1970s team jerseys, depending on your taste. The team was sponsored by Brooklyn chewing gum, an Italian brand with American-style marketing. The jersey had a blue V-shaped top, with red and white stripes below. The company name and logo, the Brooklyn Bridge, was emblazoned on the chest. The jersey was distinctive, and so were the riders Brooklyn sponsored.

BELGIAN FOUNDATIONS

The rider most associated with the Brooklyn jersey is Roger De Vlaeminck, "Mr. Paris–Roubaix," the four-time winner of that great race. But others include Patrick Sercu, Giancarlo Bellini, and Johan De Muynck. Brooklyn had quite a few Belgians. The 1970s was a golden time for Belgian cycling. It had Eddy Merckx of course, and also

Few jerseys have come up to the design standards of the Brooklyn team. It's still popular today, with replica Brooklyn jerseys a big favorite of retro cycling fans.

Roger De Vlaeminck wearing the green jersey of the 1970 Tour de France. He also won a stage in the race that year.

Roger De Vlaeminck and Walter Godefroot, and others won plenty of races. Italian manufacturing was doing well, but the Italian currency, the lira, wasn't strong, especially compared to the Belgian franc. For good Belgian racers an Italian contract was the key to prosperity. Merckx went to Faema in 1969, Godefroot to Salvarani in 1970, and De Vlaeminck to Dreher in 1972. Then in 1973 he transferred to Brooklyn for the entire life of the team.

De Vlaeminck won Paris–Roubaix three times for Brooklyn, plus Il Lombardia twice, and Milan–San Remo and the Tour of Flanders once each. He gave the company a huge return, but so did Patrick Sercu, who won the green jersey in the 1974 Tour de France, and Giancarlo Bellini, who won the King of the Mountains title in the 1976 Tour.

Brooklyn raced on Gios bikes, painted the same perfect blue as their jerseys. It was a classy package made classier by De Vlaeminck's elegant riding. No matter how rough the road surface, De Vlaeminck seemed to float effortlessly over it. It has become the stuff of myth and legend, although it certainly wasn't as effortless as it looked.

Johan De Muynck was another Belgian who made the Brooklyn jersey look good. He finished second overall in the 1978 Giro d'Italia, which caused ripples in pro cycling at the time. De Muynck was hired to help Roger De Vlaeminck in his efforts to win the Giro d'Italia. Although a Classics specialist, De Vlaeminck won several good stage races, including the very mountainous Tour of Switzerland in 1975. The Tour de France was impossible for him because he always had a full Classics season, and because he rode for Italian teams, so he always had to ride the Giro. The Tour was a race too far, but the Giro wasn't. However, in 1976 De Muynck was better than De Vlaeminck, so he started riding for himself. That didn't go down too well with De Vlaeminck, and De Muynck left the team. In 1978 De Muynck won the Giro d'Italia for Bianchi, proving he was a better Grand Tour rider than Roger De Vlaeminck.

TI-Raleigh

1972-1983

In 1972 the Nottingham-based bike manufacturer launched a sales drive in Europe. Sponsorship of a pro team formed part of the campaign, and Raleigh dipped its toe in the water in 1972 and 1973 with a team of British racers under British management. At that time, though, there was a huge gulf between professional racing in the UK and in continental Europe. The team was out of its depth in terms of experience and finance. It needed to go up a gear in both.

PETER THE GREAT

Raleigh gave the job of getting the team off the ground to David Duffield. It was his decision to hire a Dutchman, Peter Post, as team manager for 1974. Post had been a great racer, the winner of the 1964 Paris–Roubaix at what is still the record speed for that race, and a superb six-day racer. "I commentated at the Skol Six-Day, so I'd seen Peter work as a rider, and when he became the race director. I can sum up what I thought about him leading the Raleigh team by saying he was a winner, I'd seen that, but he also had something else. He was a tough racer, and he was respected for it, but he had a certain something, a natural authority if you like. I just thought that here was a man who would be equal to any challenge," Duffield told *Cycle Sport* magazine in 2011.

Peter Post winning a stage of the 1960s Tour of Holland. He later won several big road races, including Paris–Roubaix in 1964, and became the top six-day racer of his generation.

Belgian Paul Wellens leads
teammate Joop Zoetemelk on
the 17th stage of the 1980 Tour
de France, which Zoetemelk
won for TI-Raleigh.

"I didn't do it because they were bad riders, I just needed to get into their heads what European racing was about, what a pro team was about. It's not about individuals trying their best and trusting to luck. It's about having a plan and executing it so you win the race. Barras was very good, very fast, but he didn't have the right attitude and I couldn't change him," Post said in an interview in 2006. Post was hard on anybody he saw as different to his model of what a pro cyclist should be. But it worked; he created an all-conquering team that won the Tour de France, world titles, and many Classics. And a lot of that team thought Peter Post was the greatest team manager ever and were unswervingly loyal.

The man who displayed most loyalty to Post was someone whom he described once as the perfect professional, Henk Lubberding. "He asked for loyalty but in return Post did everything for his riders. He paid us well. He got contracts for critériums for the guys who helped, as well as the team's winners. He got the best equipment, arguing with suppliers for it and sending back anything that was no good. Post's teams had a good reputation among the pros, and for all those who criticized him there were ten who would have gladly raced for him," says Lubberding, who spent all of his 11-year pro career in Post's teams.

So Post took over and, basing the whole team in mainland Europe, brought in some Dutch riders and began to get rid of the Brits. This despite the fact that they were good, with the potential to be better—Phil Bayton, for example, had finished fourth in the 1972 Olympic Games road race. And Sid Barras was a superfast sprinter who won a stage of the Tour of Switzerland while racing for a small British team. Post was hard on the Brits, overhard, goading them into stand-up arguments at the dinner table, but he says he had a reason.

The TI-Raleigh team had a number of different cosponsors, and each one prompted changes in the jersey design. However, once this design was chosen in 1974, it was retained for the remainder of the team's life.

THE JERSEY

The TI-Raleigh jersey wouldn't look out of place in the pro peloton today. Indeed, the British-based Raleigh pro team race today in a very similar jersey to TI-Raleigh. It looked smart, very professional, and no-nonsense. As such, the jersey reflected the values of the TI-Raleigh team at its best. TI stands for Tube Investments, which at the time was Raleigh's parent company.

The team had a number of cosponsors, including the white goods manufacturer Creda and an American sportswear brand, McGregor. Not only was the jersey very modern, TI Raleigh was the first team to race in Lycra bib-shorts. Its jerseys were wool at first, but became a wool–manmade fiber mix as the 1970s ticked over into the 1980s.

Raleigh's Tour

The stated aim at the outset of the TI-Raleigh team was victory in the Tour de France on a Raleigh bike. Ideally, that victory would be with a British rider, but that wasn't going to happen, not at that time in pro cycling. In the end, predictably, it was a Dutchman who won for Raleigh. Joop Zoetemelk was one of the best stage racers around, and Post signed him specifically because of his Tour-winning potential.

Zoetemelk was second to Eddy Merckx in the 1971 Tour, but he had a bad crash in 1973, and his subsequent recovery was slow. He finished second in the 1976 Tour, and again in 1978 and 1979. Zoetemelk's eventual win came at the expense of the man who beat him in those last two Tours, Bernard Hinault. It looked like Hinault would win in 1980, when he dominated a stage from Liège to Lille that went over some of the cobbled sectors of Paris-Roubaix. It was stage five, part of a very hard first week, and it rained. Hinault out-sprinted Hennie Kuiper, resulting in a two-minute lead over of the rest. However, Hinault developed tendonitis in his knee during the stage, and although he kept going through the next few days, Zoetemelk closed in on him.

By stage 12 Hinault decided he had no alternative but to quit while wearing the yellow jersey. They would hit the Alps next day, and Hinault could have damaged his knee permanently if he continued. With nobody to challenge him, Zoetemelk took over and cruised to victory in Paris. TI-Raleigh's mission statement had been delivered.

Some say Zoetemelk's 1980 Tour de France win was due to Bernard Hinault dropping out, but that's unfair. The fact is, Zoetemelk finished the race and Hinault couldn't.

Bernard Hinault riding for La Vie Claire at the 1985 Coors Classic. An iconic rider in an iconic jersey.

CHAPTER 10

THE 1980s—A DECADE OF REVOLUTION

The 1980s was a period of change in cycling, when the aerodynamics of cycling were better understood and bikes and clothing adapted to reduce air resistance. This didn't have too much effect on road race jerseys at first, although skinsuits were widely used in time trials, where good aerodynamics are crucial. The decade also saw the end of the wool jersey.

Skil-Sem

1984–1985

Skil-Sem was Sean Kelly's team when the great Irish rider was at the height of his career. He was the world's number one cyclist, and he not only inspired loyalty from a team that had been built around him, he also inspired other members, like Gerrie Knetemann, Jörg Müller, and Jean-Claude Leclercq, to great victories for the team.

LE VICOMTE

Jean de Gribaldy created the Skill-Sem team for his protégé Sean Kelly. De Gribaldy was known in French cycling as *le Vicomte*, "the Viscount." He didn't actually hold a title, but he was a descendent of the aristocratic Italian Broglia family. No money came with the de Gribaldy name; the son of a farmer, Jean qualified as a clock repairer, but his heart lay in cycling. He wasn't a huge success, but he achieved his ambition. He rode the Tour de France twice, was second in the 1947 French road race championship, and took top-ten placings in Milan–San Remo and Liège–Bastogne–Liège.

This Skil jersey, with four sponsors represented on it, shows how rules pertaining to the number of sponsors a team could carry on its clothing had changed by the 1980s.

Sean Kelly of Ireland was the best of Jean de Gribaldy's protégés, and Kelly says that de Gribaldy was his best manager.

After he retired, de Gribaldy opened a store in Besançon, France, which he built into a small department store, selling bikes, scooters, kitchen appliances, and TV sets. By 1968 it had grown big enough for de Gribaldy to sponsor and manage his own pro team, which he did with several cosponsors, Hoover, Frimatic, Magniflex, and Miko. He even persuaded the rich widow of a Greek millionaire, Miriam De Kova, to cosponsor a team with him. De Gribaldy also had a knack for discovering talent outside the mainstream cycling

countries. He brought a Portuguese ex-soldier called Joaquim Agostinho into pro cycling, as he did for the Danish amateur world pursuit champion Mogens Frey. They both won stages in the Tour de France. His knack wasn't entirely altruistic; de Gribaldy knew that foreigners asked for less money than Frenchmen. Sean Kelly, however, broke that particular mold.

After seeing Kelly's name a lot in the results when Kelly raced as an amateur in France in 1976, de Gribaldy flew in his 12-seater private plane to Ireland then took a taxi to the Kelly family farm, where he found Sean driving a tractor. He offered Kelly a contract with the French side of the Flandria team, which de Gribaldy was putting together. Kelly hesitated; turning pro was a big deal back then—only a handful of Irish riders had done it. De Gribaldy improved the offer, and Kelly said he would think about it. The offer was upped again in the meantime, and three weeks later the Irish rider signed his first pro contract.

Although he was signed for the French side of Flandria, Kelly was so good he ended up racing for the first team, which was the Belgian side. From 1979 until 1981 he raced for another Belgian team, Splendor. De Gribaldy had less to do with him until 1982, when he thought Kelly was ready to be a team leader. De Gribaldy created the Sem-France Loire team for him, Kelly began winning big, and the power tool company Skil took over as headline sponsor in 1984.

THE JERSEY

The colors of the Skil-Sem jersey were the same as those of the main sponsor Skil. In 1984, Sem was one of three cosponsors on the jersey, alongside Reydel, which designs motor car interiors, and the French bike equipment manufacturer Mavic. The jersey's side panel was blue, a nod to the corporate colors of Kas, the company belonging to de Gribaldy's Spanish friend Louis Knorr, whom de Gribaldy hoped to get involved in team sponsorship again. That happened in 1985, when Kas appeared with Miko on the Skil-Sem jersey side panel, then took over as headline sponsor of the team in 1986.

Skil returned to cycling sponsorship as the Skil-Shimano team in 2010, with jerseys quite similar to those worn by its team in the 1980s. The company also sponsored a women's team, with slightly different jerseys, with green stripes replacing the diagonal red ones of Skil-Sem and Skil-Shimano.

KELLY'S HOT STREAK

The exploit most keenly associated with the Skil jersey took place over two weeks in April 1984. Having lost the Tour of Flanders through a miscalculation on the first Sunday of that fortnight, April 1, Sean Kelly flew to Spain and the next day started in the Tour of the Basque Country. Despite treating the race as a training exercise, he still won four stages and took overall victory. On Friday, April 6, Kelly flew to Paris, where, on Sunday, April 8, he started in the Paris–Roubaix. He was flying.

Conditions were terrible in 1984; the cobbles were wet and slick with mud. A local rider, Alain Bondue, knew what to expect and attacked on the run-in to Arenberg, a notorious stretch of road through Arenberg Forest. He hit the cobbles first, and behind him there was mayhem, as riders slipped and fell. Kelly ploughed through it all untouched. Out of Arenberg, he dropped back to the Skil team car to consult with de Gribaldy, who

The modern Skil-Shimano team at a pre-race presentation in 2010.

Sean Kelly, second right, wins the 1983 Tour de France green jersey. This was when Sem was the headline sponsor of the team, with Mavic as a cosponsor.

advised caution, but caution had cost Kelly races, so he decided to take matters into his own hands and go after the leaders himself. He did so on a stretch of cobbles, and although the others reacted, only Rudy Rogiers of Belgium could follow. Kelly caught and passed everybody, including Bondue, then easily outsprinted Rogiers on the velodrome in Roubaix.

Kelly rode La Flèche Wallonne in the middle of the following week, then lined up for Liège–Bastogne–Liège on Sunday, April 15, and won that race in masterful fashion. In the space of 14 days, Kelly finished second in Flanders, won the overall and three stages of the Tour of the Basque country, then won Paris–Roubaix and Liège–Bastogne–Liège. That's a winning sequence of a hilly stage race, cobbled Classic, and hilly Classic. It was Merckx-esque, and we probably won't see the like of it again.

Six seconds

Six seconds is the narrowest ever margin of victory in any Grand Tour. It was achieved in the 1984 Vuelta a España by the Skil rider Éric Caritoux, who hadn't even known he would be riding until the day before. The Skil team manager, Jean de Gribaldy, was a great in many respects, but he wasn't the most organized person in cycling. Close to the start of the Vuelta, race organizers had to remind him that he was due to send a team. It took him several days to get enough riders together to take part for Skil. The last of them was the French second-year pro, Caritoux, whom de Gribaldy contacted the day before the race.

Del Tongo

1982-1991

Created by manager Pietro Algeri in 1982, Del Tongo was home to some of the best Italian riders of their generation. The management setup had a year out after Del Tongo pulled out of cycling sponsorship, then came back with another great team, MG Maglificio, in 1992. That team begat the Mapei superteam of the 1990s.

Del Tongo is a kitchen company, and its team's stylish yellow jersey matched the style of the products it sold. The jerseys were made by Santini, and were at their most elegant at the beginning of the team's history, when it was called Del Tongo-Colnago. Those jerseys were a rich yellow with black collars and cuffs, and a black side panel that extended over the shoulders. The text of the Del Tongo logo was lower case, and the Colnago cloverleaf trademark was sometimes inside the capital C of Colnago. All writing was black.

One of the later Del Tongo jerseys. Due to an increasing number of sponsors, the design was by this stage beginning to lose the lines of its original style.

Giuseppe Saronni gets a pat on the back from French movie star Alain Delon, who was a guest of the organizers for the seventh stage of the 1987 Tour de France.

At first the team rode flame-red Colnago Mexico bikes with chrome head lugs and chrome forks, and most of the rear triangle was chrome-plated. They were fancy, but still quite beautiful bikes. Their desirability was increased dramatically by the star of the Del Tongo team, Giuseppe Saronni. He gave Del Tongo the rainbow jersey in its first year of team sponsorship, when a scintillating attack right at the end of a hard race on a circuit in the South Downs, in southern England, brought him the title. He then won the 1983 Giro d'Italia, his second Giro victory. He also won Milan–San Remo in 1983. It is very special for an Italian to win wearing the rainbow jersey, but Saronni had gone one better by winning Il Lombardia in the rainbow colors the previous year.

Saronni's performances dropped after 1983, but Gianbattista Baronchelli won Il Lombardia for Del Tongo in 1986, and Franco Ballerini won the 1990 GP of America, which the UCI was trying to promote to a Classic at that time. Maurizio

Fondriest was the other big name in the Del Tongo team. He was the other rider to give the team the rainbow jersey when he transferred from Alfa Lum-Ecoflam at the end of 1988. Fondriest was only 23, and was the surprise winner of the 1988 world road race title in Ronse, Belgium. Two of the favorites, Steve Bauer of Canada and the home country's Claude Criquielion, had collided, resulting in a bad crash for the Belgian, which made Fondriest's task slightly easier.

Later, the addition of extra sponsors to the Del Tongo jersey affected its style— some would say adversely—but the team gave the new sponsors great value for money when it signed a new pro from Tuscany in 1989. Mario Cipollini rapidly became one of the best sprinters in cycling. He was one of the first of the modern era—sprinters who could increase their velocity at the end of their high-speed lead-out trains, and maintain that speed all the way to the line.

La Vie Claire

1984–1986

La Vie Claire was a revolutionary team—from the salary it paid, the methods and philosophy of its Swiss team manager, Paul Koechli, through to the design of its jersey and the equipment the team used. It was one of the first teams to use carbon-fiber frames, and one of the first to use the revolutionary Look clipless pedals. It was also a very good team, with two Tour de France wins in its first three years, but that was because it hired the best two riders, Bernard Hinault and Greg LeMond.

Bernard Hinault in the Celestial Seasonings version of the La Vie Claire jersey. Celestial Seasonings is an American tea brand that sponsored La Vie Claire for U.S. races.

THE JERSEY

An absolute classic, the La Vie Claire jersey was designed by Benetton and based on a work of art by the Dutch painter Piet Mondrian—*Composition With Large Red Pane, Yellow, Black, Gray, and Blue* (1921). It is a quite faithful representation, with a large pane of red and the other colors in a grid of black lines. The jersey's design fit with the style of the 1980s, but it is timeless as well. The painting is influential still, and lucrative—you can buy a smartphone cover that imitates the famous work.

La Vie Claire is a health-food company that was owned by millionaire businessman and budding politician Bernard Tapie. In its first year, the team was cosponsored by Terraillon, which at the time made kitchen scales and was also owned by Tapie. In subsequent years, other names from the growing portfolio of businesses he owned featured on the jerseys, notably Wonder, Radar, and Look.

Is this the best-designed cycling jersey ever? A lot of people think so. It was groundbreaking in its day, and it still looks good now.

THE TEAM

There was big publicity over Greg LeMond's deal with Bernard Tapie to join La Vie Claire in 1985, where Bernard Hinault had been the top rider. It was said to be the first million-dollar contract in cycling. It was paid in three stages over three years, and it represented a step-change in the amount cyclists were paid. Thanks to the contract, every pro rider's value increased.

LeMond didn't really want to leave Renault-Elf. His manager there, Cyrille Guimard, had nurtured LeMond, and LeMond was still only 23. He'd already been world champion and finished third

in the Tour de France, and he could have continued to benefit from guidance by somebody he could trust—something he would lack at La Vie Claire.

Bernard Hinault was happy with LeMond's move. He wanted to win at least one more Tour de France, and he had worked hard to regain his strength after missing the 1983 Tour through injury. By the start of 1985, Hinault was back to something like his normal self. He was confident of winning again, and having LeMond in the same team was good for him. It would leave the 1983 and '84

Laurent Fignon winning stage 20 of the 1989 Giro d'Italia, which he also won overall.

Tour winner, Laurent Fignon, with a dilemma, because La Vie Claire had two tactical options to play. Fignon dominated the 1984 Tour de France, in which Hinault was making his way back. Now, a full-strength Bernard Hinault, and a Greg LeMond with another year's strength and experience, would be a tough proposition for Fignon.

A TALE OF TWO TOURS

Bernard Hinault and Greg LeMond were head and shoulders above the rest in the 1985 and 1986 Tours de France. Hinault won in 1985, with LeMond second, and those positions reversed the following year. All very good, you might think. But no, it wasn't.

LeMond says he held back to let Hinault win in 1985. He even says that on one stage he was given wrong information by the La Vie Claire management, which was designed to hold him back. Despite this, he remained sanguine about Hinault's victory because he believed they had a deal. Any serenity LeMond may have felt was dispelled the following year, however, when Hinault attacked him and took the yellow jersey early on. LeMond said that Hinault had gone back on his word by attacking. Hinault said he was attacking to sap their rivals' strength, and it wasn't his fault if LeMond couldn't see that.

In the end, LeMond won, proving he was the stronger that year, but the dispute about what had taken place rumbled on for a long time after. Thankfully, it's all water under the bridge for them now.

Who is Bernard Tapie?

Bernard Tapie, now 73, had an eventful life to say the least. He became a multimillionaire by buying businesses, getting them to flourish, then selling at a profit. His first acquisition was the battery manufacturer Leclanché-Wonder. In 1980, he bought La Vie Claire, in 1986 he became president of the French soccer team Olympique de Marseille, and in 1989 he was elected to the French Assembly for the Bouches-du-Rhône constituency. A member of the Radical Party of the Left, he rose in the governments of President François Mitterrand to be Minister of City Affairs.

Tapie was a minister between April 1992 and March 1993, at which time he was embroiled in accusations of match-fixing during a game between Marseille and Valenciennes. In 1994, he was put under investigation for complicity in corruption, and he was eventually convicted and sentenced to two years in prison, serving eight months.

Bernard Tapie (center) poses with his star riders, Bernard Hinault (left) and Greg LeMond.

Carrera

The Carrera team was at the forefront of innovation in cycling clothing during the second half of the 1980s, when wool changed to manmade Lycra mixes. Lycra is lighter and easier to manufacture and care for, and is also more suited to the application of wording and patterns. While wool is good at moving moisture away from the body, manmade fibers are even better. They can also be made more form-fitting, and therefore more aerodynamic.

DENIM STYLE

The ease of creating patterned Lycra (and other manmade materials) is illustrated by Carrera's team kit. Carrera is a manufacturer of denim jeans, and, after starting with black Lycra shorts, by the 1990s the team's shorts were denim-effect blue Lycra, with a stitching effect in the pattern to make it look as though the riders were wearing cut-off jeans. The blue panel on the team's jersey also got the "denim-look" treatment.

A Carrera jersey showing the mock denim side panels. This version of the team jersey is from the early 1990s.

Stephen Roche in the crucial stage ten time trial of the 1987 Tour de France from Saumur to Futuroscope, which he won, thus laying the foundations for overall victory.

The team started life as Carrera-Inoxpran and won the Giro d'Italia with Roberto Visentini in 1986, the year that Irish rider Stephen Roche joined. Roche had a poor year in 1986, when the team changed to Carrera Jeans-Vagabond, but in 1987 Roche raced like he was in a state of grace. He won cycling's Triple Crown, taking the Giro d'Italia, Tour de France, and world road race title in the same year. Only Eddy Merckx had done it before, and nobody has done it since.

When Roche raced for Carrera, the team had Peugeot on their shorts. It was the result of a dispute he'd had with his first team since 1983. He had agreed in principle to stay with Peugeot, but they couldn't agree on money. Another French team, La Redoute, could match his demands, so Roche signed for them in 1984. That resulted in a protracted dispute with Peugeot that went on for months. The upshot was that Roche and Carrera had to carry the Peugeot name on their shorts when Roche did the 1987 Triple Crown. Incidentally, shorts

lettering had changed by that point, so the Peugeot name ran vertically down each leg. TI-Raleigh had introduced that layout some years before.

Roche left Carrera in 1988, only to return for his last two years as a pro. A subsequent Carrera star was Claudio Chiappucci; however, although Chiappucci won events, including King of the Mountains titles in the Giro d'Italia and the Tour de France, he didn't quite get the top spot in a Grand Tour. It was fascinating watching him try, though, because he had a flair for long, lone, often doomed, attacks.

The same is true of the next Carrera star, Marco Pantani, although Pantani's attacks produced greater success. His talent emerged with Carrera between 1992 and 1996, although he had his biggest wins later with other teams. The small-statured Pantani's lightning progress was derailed by the revelations of doping so commonplace in the late 1990s and early 2000s Grand Tours. Pantani died from a cocaine overdose in 2004.

Z

Early in 1987, the year following his historic first American Tour de France victory, Greg LeMond was shot in a hunting accident and nearly died. His rehabilitation was long, hard, and fraught with setbacks, but he finally won his second Tour de France in 1989. A few weeks later, LeMond won his second world road race title. He was back where he had been, the hottest property in cycling, and one team above all others wanted to buy him.

Robert Millar on the lower slopes of Alpe d'Huez during stage 17 of the 1991 Tour de France.

THE Z DEAL

Roger Zannier's children's clothing brand Z took over the headline sponsorship of the Peugeot team in 1988, and when Peugeot pulled out at the end of the following year, Z carried on alone. To get real value for its sponsorship buck, the team needed a big name. The biggest name at that time was Greg LeMond, and he needed a deal after he'd dropped down the pecking order into a lowly Belgian squad. After bouncing back with a Tour de France and world championship victory he could name his price.

In September 1989 it was announced that LeMond had a three-year deal worth US$5.5 million to ride with the Z team. The American 7-Eleven team wanted him too, and LeMond was inclined to sign for the Americans, but they couldn't match Z's offer. Toshiba had taken over sponsorship of LeMond's old team, La Vie Claire, and they said they could match Z, but LeMond chose Z. He seemed to get on well with Roger Zannier, and he definitely did with the team manager, Roger Legeay. LeMond liked Legeay, and Legeay really admired LeMond. He'd been the only manager of a big team to show interest in him during his fightback from injury, before the 1989 Tour de France.

Z used its store's logos to great effect on its team jerseys, so the connection between them and the team was instantly recognizable.

LeMond negotiated victory bonuses from Z for his teammates, and he had the whole deal underpinned by a bank guarantee. That was another way Greg LeMond changed professional cycling. When he signed the US$1-million deal with La Vie Claire, he dragged every other rider's worth up in his wake. It happened again with the Z deal. What's more, introducing a bank guarantee to make everyone in the team more secure was another big step forward. All top-level professional cycling teams are financed that way now.

THE JERSEY

The Z team kit was quite revolutionary. It was a bold blue-and-light-blue combination, with the comic-book-style Z logo in the middle, accompanied by the words *Vêtements Enfants* ("Children's Clothing") as explanation of the headline brand. LeMond had launched his own bike brand, so the team rode LeMond bikes, which were full of the latest technology. The team uniform looked good and was of high-quality manufacture, and the riders were well supported. The team name for 1990 was Z-Tomasso, which became Z in 1991. Z was one of the first teams to use fully zippered racing jerseys, to facilitate air circulation in very hot conditions.

Greg LeMond in the American Tour Du Pont yellow jersey. By 1992 the team's logo and name could be printed on a leader's jersey within minutes of a stage finish.

Reluctant alumni

In 2000, ten years after LeMond won his third Tour de France, and Z won the team classification by a record-breakingly narrow margin of 16 seconds, the Z team held a reunion. It was a very active one, in which the 1990 Tour team took part in l'Étape du Tour, which ended at the top of Mont Ventoux.

Not all among Z's stable of riders joined the reunion. Gilbert Duclos-Lassalle didn't attend; he told the press that it was dangerous for men of his age to go climbing mountains like Ventoux. Robert Millar was also missing. And among those that did attend, Ronan Pensec grumpily moaned from the back of their group that there was no way he was even going to start climbing the Ventoux. But Greg LeMond was there, front and center with his men, marshaling them as he had done ten years before.

A TIGHT-KNIT GROUP

LeMond's team was a special bunch, totally committed to a LeMond victory. Two thirds of the team were French, but the French—both the public and riders—never had a problem with Greg LeMond. He was a rider they could understand. He won, but it always looked as though he could lose. They liked that. And he almost did lose the 1990 Tour in the Pyrenees. It was stage 17 from Lourdes to Pau. Claudio Chiappucci had the yellow jersey, but LeMond and Z were hunting him down, stage by stage. Toward the top of the Col de Marie-Blanque, LeMond punctured, and for once he had no teammates near him.

A new wheel took an age to come, but with it came help from Éric Boyer and Jérôme Simon. They started to chase, pacing LeMond, but hadn't gone 200 yards (180 meters) before LeMond had another problem, forcing him to change bikes. At the top of the Marie-Blanque he was

1 minute 27 seconds down on Chiappucci and losing the Tour. LeMond descended like a stone, but ahead of him on the flat, Chiappucci and his team were really going for it. Roger Legeay had to ask the two Z riders who were in the leading group to drop back to help LeMond. Their reaction speaks volumes for the respect they had for Legeay and for their American team leader.

Gilbert Duclos-Lassalle and Atle Kvålsvoll almost stopped in the road. The Chiappucci group screamed past while they dawdled along, waiting for LeMond. Seventy-five seconds slipped by before he arrived. A team Z train was hitched to the front of the group that had formed around LeMond, and it hauled their leader back up to Chiappucci. It was a great moment. Three days later LeMond hammered Chiappucci in the final time trial and won the Tour de France for America and for Z, and maybe, in a little way, for France as well.

LeMond (third left) struggling in the 1991 Giro d'Italia. The effects of his hunting accident have returned, this time irreversibly, but he still has faithful Z riders with him.

The ONCE team riding the team
time trial stage of the 1995
Tour de France. The team was
one of the biggest and best
organized of the 1990s, but it
was also heavily involved in
some of the doping scandals
of that decade.

THE 1990s—THE AGE OF THE SUPERTEAM

An advance in printing technology gave designers much more scope for creativity, allowing them to move beyond the simple branding of previous jerseys. The 1990s was an era of large sponsors and bigger teams, which reflected the increasing specialization of pro cycling, with riders increasingly excelling in either Grand Tours or the Classics.

Mapei

Pro cycling became more specialized during the 1990s. The 1985 Tour winner, Bernard Hinault, regularly won the biggest single-day races, the Monuments, as well as the Grand Tours, but nobody has done so to his extent since. After Greg LeMond's era, it was very rare for a Grand Tour winner to even ride the gnarlier single-day races, the cobbled Classics. So to maximize publicity in this new era, teams built groups of riders around certain races. Teams got bigger to accommodate that, and had bigger budgets. If they didn't increase their sponsorship revenue, a team would be limited to competing in a narrow band of races. Mapei was one of the first teams to try to fight on all fronts.

THE DREAM TEAM

Giorgio Squinzi was the man behind Mapei. He owned the company, which makes products for the DIY and building industry, and he loved cycling for its core values, its beauty, and its soul. Squinzi was a keen cyclist. He loved Colnago bikes, and he loved meeting the riders he had admired as a youngster. He made friends with many of them, one of whom was Ercole Baldini, the 1956 Olympic and 1958 professional world road race champion. Baldini mentored an Italian pro, Marco Giovannetti, who won the 1990 Vuelta a España. Later Giovannetti began experiencing problems with his Spanish team, so Baldini asked Squinzi if his company would consider cosponsoring the team. Squinzi said yes, and when the Spanish headline sponsor, Clas, pulled out at the end of 1993, Squinzi took over the entire team.

Andrea Tafi of Italy won Paris-Roubaix (1999), Il Lombardia (1996), Tour of Flanders (2002), and the Italian road race title (1998) for Mapei.

Total dominance: the all-Mapei finish of the 1996 Paris–Roubaix. Mapei was the best team ever in this race, winning it five times in the ten years of the team's existence.

Mapei's magic moment

Mapei's standout achievement happened at the end of the 1996 Paris–Roubaix, where Mapei scored a one-two-three and provided photographers with a stunning moment. Three Mapei riders were pictured crossing the finish line, arms in the air, celebrating their team's total victory, without a single other rider in the shot.

The three Mapei riders had left the rest of the field gasping in their wake and entered the Roubaix velodrome together. But they didn't sprint. Johan Museeuw rolled over the line first, Gianluca Bortolami was second, with Andrea Tafi third. It was discovered later that the order was decided by Squinzi during a telephone call he made to the Mapei sports director during the race, while Squinzi watched on TV in Italy. The first two riders were happy with the decision, but Tafi wasn't. He did, however, come to accept what Squinzi had done, and he won Paris–Roubaix in an equally brilliant way in 1999.

Squinzi was close to his riders, and Tafi later had cause to value Squinzi's friendship and loyalty when, after a bad year in 2001, with no results because of nerve damage in his left leg, Tafi's career looked over. With his Mapei contract coming to an end, and no one else interested, Squinzi asked Tafi if, at nearly 36, he really wanted to go on. When Tafi said he did, Squinzi kept him in the team at no reduction in pay.

When he pulled out of team sponsorship, Squinzi admitted that some of his riders were more than employees to him, they were friends. He said that Franco Ballerini's 1995 and 1998 Paris–Roubaix wins were the most emotional moments of his entire sponsorship experience, adding, "With Franco I have a special friendship which goes beyond our professional relationship."

The Clas team had a very good rider in Tony Rominger, and Squinzi signed emerging talents like Abraham Olano and Gianluca Bortolami. Mapei was an instant success, hitting number one in the UCI team rankings by the end of 1994, and Bortolami won the UCI World Cup and Rominger the Vuelta a España. Rominger also shocked experts by taking the World Hour Record at the end of the season, despite being a track-racing novice. The team welded together Spanish and Italian riders to make a squad that could fight on some fronts, but not all. This changed in 1995, when Mapei amalgamated with the Belgian GB-MG squad to form a superteam. It was the first team ever to be staffed and run as the biggest teams are today.

So in 1995 Squinzi had a team that could take on anyone in anything, anywhere, with riders like Johan Museeuw and Frank Vandenbroucke and another close friend of Squinzi's, Franco Ballerini, adding Classics firepower to the stage race capabilities of Rominger and Olano. Rominger won the 1995 Giro d'Italia; however, after he left the team, Mapei didn't win another Grand Tour, and that gave Squinzi pause for thought. After setting up a Mapei training center with great coaches, the best facilities, and still failing to win a Grand Tour, he came to the conclusion that it was impossible for riders to win Grand Tours without doping. Squinzi pulled Mapei out of team sponsorship at the end of 2002, saying, "I feel defeated by the curse of doping. I tried everything I could to overcome this evil, to make cycling credible and respectable again, but I lost."

Tony Rominger took Mapei's only Grand Tour victories, the Vuelta a España in 1994 and the Giro d'Italia in 1995.

This is the 1995 Mapei-GB jersey. GB is a chain of Belgian supermarkets. This Italo-Belgian squad was the grandfather of the Etixx-Quick Step team today.

THE JERSEY

The Mapei jersey changed over the years, depending on the cosponsor. A constant feature, though, was the multicolored cubes on every version. They were a designer's depiction of the raw plastic granules that went into Mapei's colored adhesives and floor coverings. They were usually set against a blue background, although in 1998 the jersey background was changed to white, to reflect the branding of cosponsor Bricobi, a lawnmower manufacturer.

The team became Mapei-Quick Step in 1999, bringing in one of the most recognizable sponsors in pro cycling today. If the Mapei-Bricobi jerseys had been a bit fussy, with the addition of blue swirled lines as well as multicolored cubes, the Mapei-Quick Step jersey was very smart. The colored cubes grew not just in size but also in style, making them look more integrated into the overall design.

ONCE

Spanish team ONCE revolutionized the way riders trained, breaking the season up and doing a training camp after the Spring Classics each year. Before that, riders attended one pre-season camp, then raced more or less all year. Most teams now do blocks of training throughout the racing calendar, with training structured more carefully to maximize gains. Training blocks are a surer way to build to peak fitness for a specific target race.

Of course it's possible that more than just training went on at some of the camps, especially in the light of the arrest of ONCE's principal manager, Manolo Saiz, on suspicion of doping. Nevertheless, the ONCE team's practices represented a step up in professionalism, as was the clothing the riders wore. It was supplied by the Basque clothing company Etxeondo, and it looked superb. The company was founded by Francisco Rodrigo, who started his career working in sublimation, a printing technique, with clients that included the fashion houses Dior and Balenciaga.

The ONCE jersey in its pink Tour de France incarnation. This example is from when the jersey was beginning to get cluttered with sponsors' names and logos.

ONCE riders prepare for a team time trial in the Tour de France. Johan Bruyneel, second left, became famous after his racing career as Lance Armstrong's team manager.

He loved cycling, and in 1976 he founded his company in the village of Etxeondo, near San Sebastián. Rodrigo's knowledge of style and craftsmanship is clear in Etxeondo's products, and it was certainly clear in the simple stylings of the ONCE team jersey.

ONCE is a Spanish lottery for the blind and visually impaired. Over 85 percent of its staff are disabled, and 40 percent are over 65. The ONCE team jersey was yellow, with a stylized silhouette of a person walking with a cane on the front of it. The figure was repeated on collar and cuffs, and the name "ONCE" was on the front, back, and shoulders of the jersey. In early versions, there was a wide panel on each side of the jersey, which narrowed over the shoulders. Because it was mostly yellow, the team had to change its jersey color for the Tour de France. It chose pink—a choice that didn't quite work on the style front.

The 1989 to 1998 versions of the ONCE jersey were the most simple and the most stylish. Later, as the team got cosponsors, such as Deutsche Bank and Eroski, the jersey had to be changed to accommodate their logos, and it lost some of its style. When ONCE pulled out of cycling at the end of 2003, because by then everybody in Spain knew the name, Manolo Saiz got Liberty Seguros to sponsor his team, which became Liberty Seguros-Würth in 2005 and just Würth in 2006. But by then Manolo Saiz had been arrested in connection with the Operation Puerto doping scandal. Saiz resigned, and his management company (most top pro teams are owned by management companies now) was stripped of its Pro Tour licence. Only a finite number of Pro Tour licences are awarded each year, and Saiz's was given to the company behind the Astana team for 2007.

Banesto

1990-2003

Banesto is a bank that sponsored one of Spain's best-known teams, which started life as Reynolds in 1980 and is the Movistar team today. It is the work of José Miguel Echavarri, a former pro rider who has been far more successful at running pro teams. His teams have won a lot, and Movistar is winning still. His greatest rider was Miguel Indurain, who started with Reynolds and won five consecutive Tours de France for Banesto.

ROUGH DIAMOND

Miguel Indurain *was* Banesto. He grew up in Navarra, in the Basque region of Spain, the epitome of a big strong boy. The son of a farmer, he was a natural on a bike, so long as the race didn't go uphill. His weakness as a climber wasn't apparent during his time as an amateur because Indurain generated so much power he flattened hills and still won, but as a pro, where the standard is much higher, it was a problem.

Echavarri knew he had a diamond, but it had to be cut down and polished. He weaned Indurain off his love of home cooking and cakes, and by the time the boy became a man he had lost weight but retained his physical capacities. He had one of the biggest lung capacities. At rest, his heart beat only 28 to 30 times per minute—the lowest human heart rate ever recorded. He was tall, strong, and a near-perfect time

Miguel Indurain in a Spanish post-Tour de France exhibition race, the Criterium Ciutat de l'Hospitalet.

The Nalini version of the Banesto team jerseys with red and yellow swirling echoes of the Spanish flag on it.

trialist, a format in which power counts. Once he had lost the excess weight, his power-to-weight ratio improved, and although Indurain never attacked in the mountains, he could hang in there with the best. That's how he became the first rider in history to win the Tour de France five times in a row. Indurain ended his cycling career during the 1996 Vuelta a España, after suffering his first Tour de France defeat since 1991. The Banesto team carried on after Indurain retired, winning the Vuelta in 1998 with Abraham Olano.

The Banesto jersey changed subtly almost every year of the bank's sponsorship. An early version, with black side panels, was probably the best. It's no coincidence that it was designed and made by Etxeondo. Later,

Nalini versions, with a brushstroke of the red and yellow Spanish national flag on them, were good too. Between 2001 and 2003, the team was called iBanesto, to promote the bank's online banking service. With this, the jersey design changed radically, to predominantly blue with a white chest above an orange swoosh. They had one orange sleeve too.

In 2004 and 2005 Banesto cosponsored a team with Illes Balears, the tourist board of the Balearic islands to advertise the region. When Banesto pulled out, another bank, Caisse d'Épargne, took its place. That sponsorship lasted until 2010, when Spanish telecoms company Movistar took over. Movistar is one of the best teams in the world Tour today.

Motorola

The Motorola team emerged from an American cycling project started in 1981 by Jim Ochowicz. It was designed to give the best US riders a platform to work on before the 1984 Olympics in Los Angeles, but it became America's first successful team in world cycling. Motorola was also the launchpad of that great American dream gone wrong, Lance Armstrong.

The American national cycling team, with the backing of convenience store chain 7-Eleven, dominated cycling at the 1984 Olympics. Afterwards Jim Ochowicz decided to take the project further. "I wanted to see an American team in the top European road races, but I needed a cosponsor and I got one in the form of an Italian company Hoonved, who had already

The Motorola jersey with cosponsors Kellogg's, Polar, Eddy Merckx, and American Airlines.

been involved in cycling," Ochowicz said in 2006. Italian backing brought the 7-Eleven team a place in the 1985 Giro d'Italia. The riders had a hard spring in Europe, and things weren't going much better when the Giro started, but then Ron Kiefel and Andy Hampsten both won stages. 7-Eleven was on its way.

The team still had a tough learning curve, and it was made even harder by the time constraints Ochowicz knew were on him. "7-Eleven was kind of dragged along by the momentum, it wasn't getting a direct benefit from us racing in Europe, although it got a lot of residual publicity. Still, I knew that I had to keep the momentum going, so we had to get into the world's biggest bike race, the Tour de France, as soon as possible," he says. They achieved this in 1986, and it was a turning point in Tour de France history. Greg LeMond won the race, although he was with the French team La Vie Claire, and 7-Eleven made its mark. Its riders Alex Stieda and Davis Phinney wore the yellow jersey and both won a stage early in the race.

Motorola was allowed to cross the finish line of stage 16 of the 1995 Tour de France together out of respect for their teammate, Fabio Casartelli, who had died the previous day.

The team built on that good start, with Andy Hampsten winning the 1988 Giro d'Italia. Then the telecommunications company Motorola took over sponsorship in 1991. The team's bike sponsor, Eddy Merckx, continued under Motorola, and the team's jersey and bikes changed from 7-Eleven's red, white, and green to Motorola's distinctive blue and red livery. The Australian rider Phil Anderson was the star of Motorola in its first year, but immediately after the 1992 Olympics in Barcelona a young Texan prodigy, an excellent triathlete who was a superb cyclist, and who had decided to focus solely on cycling, joined the team. His name was Lance Armstrong.

Armstrong's 1993 world road race title, his Tour de France stage victories in 1993 and 1995, and his wins in Clásica a San Sebastián in 1995 and La Flèche Wallonne in 1996 were all achieved for the Motorola team. They are now some of the few victories that cycling's governing body, the UCI, allowed Armstrong to keep after the wide-ranging United States Anti-Doping Agency enquiry into his career.

Riders in the Dutch Lotto Jumbo team at the 2015 Tour de France wearing the very latest cycling jerseys. The smooth materials and absence of creases show how advanced cycling clothing is now in terms of aerodynamics.

MODERN JERSEYS

Modern cycling jerseys are highly technical pieces of equipment. The use of modern materials and extensive study into how they work, and how best to apply them to cycling, have resulted in racing jerseys that are comfortable, practical, and very effective. The most advanced skinsuits and racing jerseys, designed according to the principles of aerodynamics, have helped riders achieve new levels of performance.

The Modern Skinsuit

The skinsuit was the first big step in making cycling clothing more aerodynamic. In the mid-1970s, while experimenting to improve bicycle aerodynamics, the Swiss scientist Tony Maier-Moussa discovered that Lycra was more aerodynamic than bare skin. From that discovery, he developed the one-piece shorts and jersey combination, the Lycra skinsuit, and riders started using them in track races and in road time trials, with a consequent improvement in performance.

Maier-Moussa made his discovery by working in a wind tunnel, and further work on clothing in wind tunnels has been carried out over the years to refine skinsuit design. It is now known that materials of different textures work better at different speeds, so nowadays skinsuits designed specifically for track sprinters vary quite considerably from those designed for road time trialists.

Also, the key to good skinsuit design isn't just reducing seams and creases in the material in a crouched riding position, as it used to be. It is about creating facets of the skinsuit that manage the airflow over different parts of the body. Managing airflow reduces turbulence, which cuts drag. Modern skinsuits have strategically placed seams to do that, or areas where different textures of material, such as the

An example of a modern skinsuit that utilizes Maier-Moussa's 1970s discovery that Lycra and similar materials are more aerodynamic than bare skin.

Peter Sagan during the time trial stage 19 of the 2012 Tour de France. His green jersey as the points competition leader is in fact an all-green aerodynamic skinsuit.

ribs on the shoulders and arms of a Bio-Racer skinsuit, do the same. There will be different material where the suit meets the rider's skin, so airflow over that transition is managed. And many modern skinsuits have long sleeves, which underlines Maier Moussa's original findings that Lycra is more aerodynamic than skin.

Modern skinsuits are also made to work optimally in a crouched aerodynamic tuck while cycling, so they are difficult to put on and awkward to stand up in. Skinsuits used at the top-end of the sport are very hard to put on because they are made small, so that the rider's body stretches the fabrics and removes any creases. That means they are quick to wear out, and so are discarded after a few uses.

As with everything in top-level sport, there are rules about skinsuits. The most important relates to the way the suit fits the form of the rider. This came about because in 2010 the Japanese clothing brand Pearl Izumi developed a "winged" skinsuit, in which extra material filled the angle between the rider's upper arm and back when in a crouched position. As well as improving airflow, the extra material could act as a sail in crosswind situations. Tests showed this had the effect of a measurable power gain, and the winged suits were outlawed by cycling's governing body, the UCI. Riders aren't allowed to race in skinsuits made from nonporous materials, because these are deemed to give an advantage over porous materials.

The Modern Road Race Jersey

Present day

Aerodynamic drag is the biggest force acting against a cyclist when he or she starts to increase speed. And drag rises at an increasingly disproportionate rate to speed. On its journey around a cyclist, air hitting any crease in clothing becomes turbulent, which increases drag, so reducing creases cuts drag. Lycra clothing and then Lycra skinsuits decreased riders' drag in time trials and on the track, but until a few years ago very little thought was put into improving the aerodynamics of road race clothing.

A few pioneers used skinsuits in road races. The Canadian, Alex Stieda, used one on the short stage in the 1986 Tour de France, when he became the first rider from North America to wear the yellow jersey. But skinsuits in road races got much more publicity when Mark Cavendish won the

Modern aerodynamic road race jerseys like this are often made up of several different materials and can significantly lower a rider's drag factor.

2011 world road race title in Denmark. The Great Britain team's tactic involved the team controlling the race to ensure a bunch sprint. That meant the team being on the front and riding at 28–30 miles per hour (45–48 kph) for a very long time. Wearing skinsuits allowed the team to ride at that pace at a slightly reduced power output. Over the 155+ miles (250+ km) of a world title race, it gave them a considerable energy saving.

Cavendish's victory focussed attention on improving aerodynamics for road racers. There were already aerodynamic road bikes on the market, and more followed. So did aerodynamic road race helmets, designed to achieve improved air-flow over and around the rider's body, and also through the helmet for increased cooling. Soon manufacturers were producing aerodynamic road race jerseys. Such jerseys might have a smooth front to improve airflow, and a textured back to take greater advantage of the slipstream from the rider in front, which is actually an old idea. The great Spanish motor-paced racer of the 1960s, Guillermo Timoner, used to have jerseys with a smooth silk front and a rougher wool back to help grab the slipstream of his pacing motorbike.

Wearing skinsuits in the 2011 men's elite world road race championships meant the British team saved energy, which helped their support of the race winner Mark Cavendish.

Modern aerodynamic road race jerseys also have wider cuffs, made from carefully selected material, to manage airflow over the fabric-to-skin transition. Mesh might be used in the side panels to improve ventilation, and often there will be strategically placed seams and different materials to manage airflow. A modern Castelli aerodynamic road race jersey has seven different materials in its construction.

The other factor in modern road jerseys is improved cooling. Castelli's Climber's jersey makes extensive use of different-sized mesh materials and a full-length front zip. There is even a mesh collar, although the jersey still has little touches, such as wide, smooth cuffs, to improve aerodynamics. Riders must be careful with modern materials, especially mesh, because it is quite easy for the skin under them to get sunburned. Some manufacturers combat this by making garments from sun-protective materials.

Modern World Tour Jerseys

2010s

There is no better way to see how cycling jerseys have evolved over time, from Maurice Garin's white jacket, through the woolen pullovers of early racers, the national teams of the 1930s, and the styles of the 1950s and 1960s, than to compare them with the jerseys worn by the top professional riders of today. So here are all of the jerseys of the men's and women's UCI World Tours, the pinnacle of road racing.

Cannondale Pro Cycling Team

Trek Factory Racing

Lotto Soudal

Etixx-Quick Step

Team Katusha

Movistar Team

AG2R La Mondiale

Team Lotto NL-Jumbo

BMC Racing Team

IAM Cycling

Team Giant-Alpecin

Astana Pro Team

Tinkoff

Lampre-Merida

Dimension Data

Orica Greenedge

Team Sky

FDJ

Index

Image Credits

Pages 21 right, 30, 48 below, 49, 65, 65, 73, 75 below, 78, 134, 139, 153, 165, 183, 212 © Emile Arbes

Pages 26, 28, 34, 41, 42, 46, 50, 52, 55 above, 59, 106, 130, 141, 142, 144, 148, 158, 169, 174, 177, 178, 186, 190, 193, 196, 199, 207, 208, 211 © Henk Theuns

Pages 23, 37, 68, 75 above, 81 left, 84, 85 below, 89, 90, 104, 107, 112, 119, 121, 123, 124, 126, 127, 135, 137, 138, 140, 154, 155, 156, 157, 161, 168, 170, 173, 175, 180 183 © Nationaal Archief | Creative Commons

Pages 96, 98 all images, 99 all images, 100, 101 all images: © Chris Sidwells

Pages 48 above, 71, 83, 86, 88, 108, 120, 128, 145, 159, 179, 189, 191 © AFP | Getty Images

Pages 60, 62, 152, 166, 166, 172 © Keystone France

Pages 39, 117, 125, 151, 162 © Mondadori Portfolio

Pages 32, 53, 54, 56, 217 © Radu Razvan | Shutterstock.com

Pages 38, 122, 171, 206 © Ullstein Bild | Getty Images

Pages 69, 111, 115, 195 © Universal

9	© Roger Viollet
15	© Heritage Images
20	© Popperfoto
29	© STF	AFP	Getty Images
31	© AF Fotografie	Alamy Stock Photo
35	© Hulton Archive
36 above	© Doug Pensinger	Getty Images
36 below	© lazyllama	Shutterstock.com
40	© Paul Herman	Creative Commons 3.0
43	© Sanguinez	Creative Commons
44	© Georges Seguin	Creative Commons
47	© Harlingue
51	© Franck Seguin
55 below	© Ruediger Fessel
61	© Nicola	Creative Commons
67	© Topical Press Agency
70	© Garitan	Creative Commons
72	© Tobi Seftel
76	© Jeremy-Günther-Heinz Jähnick	Creative Commons
79	© Leemage	Getty Images
81 right	© Fanny Schertzer	Creative Commons
85 above	© Rena Schild	Shutterstock.com
87	© Luca Grandinetti	Shutterstock.com
91	© Pymous	Creative Commons
92	© Bert Hardy
93	© Andrew Last	Creative Commons
97	© Ralph Morse

102	© Mitch Gunn	Shutterstock.com
103	© Brynn Lennon
109	© Bianchi
118	© Bert Hardy
131	© Getty Images
132	© Roger Viollet
136 below	© Brian Townsley	Creative Commons
146	© BastienM	Creative Commons
147	© Gerard Malie	AFP	Getty Images
149	© Popperfoto
160	© Koen Mollers
164	© Jarnoux Patrick
176	© Hulton Archive
181	© Getty Images
184	© David Madison	Getty Images
187	© Pascal Pavani
188	© tetedelacourse	Creative Commons
192	© David Madison
194	© Massimo Nicolodi	Creative Commons
197	© Jérôme Prevost
198	© Steve Selwood	Creative Commons
200	© Damian Strohmeyer
201	© Tadikoro	Creative Commons
202	© Phil Cole	Allsport
204	© Eric Houdas	Creative Commons
205	© Jérôme Prevost
209	© Steve Ryan	Creative Commons
210	© Darz Mol	Creative Commons
213	© Phil Cole	AllSport
214	© Bert de Boer	Creative Commons
216	© strenghtofframeITA	Shutterstock.com
218	© Aero Tech Designs Cyclewear http://www.aerotechdesigns.com/
219	© Dan Moeller	Shutterstock.com
221 & 222	Rights for these images belong to the pro cycling teams featured.

All other images in this book are in the public domain.

Every effort has been made to credit the copyright holders of the images used in this book. We apologize for any unintentional omissions or errors and will insert the appropriate acknowledgment to any companies or individuals in subsequent editions of the work.